HAIR TRIGGER 15

A STORY WORKSHOP ANTHOLOGY

Columbia College Fiction Writing Department   Chicago 1993

Hair Trigger 15
Copyright ©1993 Columbia College
Story Workshop is a servicemark (U.S. Patent and Trademark Office Registration
No. 1080612) of John Schultz.

Columbia College Fiction Writing Department
600 South Michigan Avenue
Chicago, Illinois 60605-1996

ISBN 0-932026-33-8

Table of Contents

Stories

Creative Non-Fiction/Essay

More Stories

Preface and Acknowledgements

Hair Trigger 15 collects prose fiction and essays written by undergraduate and graduate students in Columbia College writing classes. The writings in *Hair Trigger 15* were authored by students enrolled in Story Workshop®-taught Fiction I, II, Prose Forms, and Advanced Fiction classes. *Hair Trigger,* an annual publication of the Columbia College Fiction Writing Department, has twice won first prize as the best college literary magazine in the country, in the Coordinating Council of Literary Magazines' national competition. *Hair Trigger 3* won first prize in 1979 and *Hair Trigger 8* in 1985. The judges commented that the writing in *Hair Trigger 8* was "big, energetic, and original throughout" and "some of the best work we've seen." *Hair Trigger 12* received a Silver Crown Award from the Scholastic Press Association at Columbia University.

A wide range of content, form, and language background is available in *Hair Trigger 15*. In making selections, the student editors were forced to choose among writings of nearly equal merit. Respect for the reader, for content, for form, for point of view and language, and for vividness of telling characterizes these writings.

Hair Trigger 15 is the latest in the bloodline of such widely acclaimed anthologies as *The Story Workshop Reader, Angels in My Oven, Don't You Know There's a War On?, Hair Trigger 1-14,* and *The Best of Hair Trigger.*

Fiction Writing teacher Shawn Shiflett was chiefly responsible as Faculty Advisor for supervising undergraduate and graduate student editors in the overall selection and production process for *Hair Trigger 15*. Thanks to the student editors, who read through hundreds of submissions to *Hair Trigger,* and saw to it that each manuscript received equal treatment and consideration. Thanks to Anna Dassonville for book design, to Randy Albers, Andrew Allegretti, Ann Hemenway, Gary Johnson, and Betty Shiflett for consulting on matters affecting the student editors' complex editorial selection process, and to Deborah Roberts for copyediting, proofreading, and supervising crucial phases of production. Thanks are also due again to former President of Columbia College, Mirron Alexandroff, and to the President of Columbia College, John Duff, for their continuing encouragement of this program, and to the teachers who taught in the program during the period covered.

John Schultz
Chair
Fiction Writing Department

Shawn Shiflett
Faculty Advisor
Hair Trigger 15

Hair Trigger 15 Student Editors

William Boerman-Cornell
Serafina Chamberlin
Don Gennaro De Grazia
Wilhelmina Dunbar
Vince Kunkemueller
Harlan Reece
Jennifer Shanahan
Keturah Shaw

AN AFTERNOON OF GERMAN
AND NO CHILDREN

Tammie Bob

One day when Ruthie was five, a yellow upright piano lumbered up the narrow front staircase leading to the Kimmelman's second-floor duplex. It was strapped to the backs and foreheads of two hairy-eared, big-bellied men. Mommy snaked her torso out the front door, calling instructions down the stairs to assist the delivery. "Carefully, carefully," she admonished the groaning men. "My last piano was ruined by the Nazis." Her pretty eyelids shut for a moment, sweeping away the past twenty years. Ruthie, pressing one pigtail against Mommy's ribs, watched the piano climb like an ancient turtle, pausing on each step to gasp for air.

"Why didn't you cover the piano?" Mommy fretted downward. Behind her was a wheeled platform which almost filled the entry hallway. It was padded with blankets, waiting to ease the new arrival's passage to a prominent position in the living room, from which a treasured hutch had been deposed, just as Ruthie had had to move in with her older sister Anna last year, because the baby, Marvin, was a boy.

"They won't make it," Ruthie decided, exhausted by the men's efforts. She turned back into the apartment, where the platform blocked her way. Its rippled red blankets crested up at the edges, like a nest. She crawled into it, nestling her cheek in the padding which smelled pleasantly of dust and household chemicals. Placing one hand on the floor, she wheeled herself back and forth. "Row, row, row your boat . . ." she sang softly, feeling like baby Moses adrift in the reeds of the Nile, soon to attain royalty, as bullfrogs and dragonflies lazed nearby, bloated with humidity.

"You'll get the strings wet!" Mommy called, referring, Ruthie was sure, to the globs of sweat that dripped from the piano men's faces, spattering the green-carpeted stairs.

With two hands, Ruthie steered the platform 180 degrees, gaining a fine view of Mommy's pom-pom slippers, one of which waggled on its icicle-shaped heel. "Don't drop it!" Mommy shrieked, as a deep voice growled "O.K., now O.K., easy, easy," and Mommy leaped out of sight and the doorway filled with dark and piano men. Then, though she lay on her stomach and couldn't see it, Ruthie felt the air over her head grow black and heavy, as if an enormous mastodon, like the reconstruction she had seen with Daddy, was bearing down on her.

"Ease it, ease it," a man said. Mommy screamed, "RUTHIE!" and Ruthie, suddenly hot, was already rolling sideways, like you were supposed to do if you caught fire. Mommy kept screaming, no words, only screaming, and the rough carpet burned into Ruthie's forearm and one shoulder wedged against the wall as she landed. The air swirled, spraying dust in her face. The space next to her thudded and filled in yellow and solid as a stamped foot, creating a narrow corridor where Ruthie was trapped. The platform creaked in aftershock, like cracking bones, and from above thundered a chorus of shouting, highpitched and lowpitched. Hands clamped her shoulders, Mommy's hands, pulling Ruthie forward and up so she could shout in her face, hurting her shoulders as she eased Ruthie from the space between the wall and the piano, setting her on her feet. Mommy's face was red and distorted, and behind her, in the doorway, stood the men, also shouting. One had a dent in his forehead where the strap had been and the other wore suspenders that curved outward with his belly.

". . . could have been killed!" Mommy screamed, turning Ruthie by one shoulder and smacking her a good stinging one on the tush. Ruthie, who rarely cried, hunkered down in the corner by the coat closet, clasping her knees so that in the end she missed the great moment when the piano was installed in the living room.

Despite all this, within two weeks Ruthie was able to peck out familiar melodies with one or two fingers. Soon she added three-note chords with her left hand. This must be a musical gift, the family decided, not quite like Mozart, perhaps, but certainly more than an ordinary amount of talent! Aunts and friends crowded into the modular seating on a Sunday afternoon, and in the shadow of the new piano, they helped Mommy and Daddy explore the issues of early musical training: the wrong teacher could stifle any desire Ruthie had to play piano, perhaps professionally. While chewing warm, yeasty poppy-seed cakes that crumbled into the wiggling patterns of the Danish rug, they traced the genetic source of Ruthie's gift. Daddy, lifting a finger into steam that spiralled from eight cups of café-au-lait, recalled that a second cousin, Irma, whom he had known only slightly as a knitter of scarves and mittens, had once won concert tickets from a Dusseldorf radio station, for correctly identifying one of Wagner's "Totenkinder Lieder" on a classical music version of "Name That Tune."

"But I don't recall if she *played* an instrument," Daddy said. "I only can picture her knitting by the radio, always knitting . . . " He took off his glasses sadly.

This flimsy connection was overruled by Mommy and her aunts, who invoked the memory of their family's ambidextrous twins, Magda and Masha Kornfeld, both of whom had simultaneously studied the violin and the piano. They would amaze friends and family with performances of twin harmony, Magda's right hand bowing a violin held under Masha's chin, her left hand accompanying Masha's right on the piano. Or both twins would sit at the piano fiddling their chin-held violins while using their free hands to form one complete pianist between the two of them. Mommy climbed a step stool in the front hall closet to bring down the old albums because she thought she had a picture of the twins, and there was much thumbing and flipping through the overstuffed photo albums. "I keep meaning to make order!" Mommy exclaimed, as loose mounting corners and extraneous snapshots showered around her legs. "Some I can barely identify anymore," she added, wrinkling her forehead over a brownish print of a woman obscured by furs and sloping brimmed hat.

"The twins!" Aunt Cidi exclaimed, having found Magda and Masha among twenty or so people seated around a Passover Seder table crammed with dirty dishes and wine goblets and chicken carcasses and fish bones and lumps and puddles of other food remains. There was a grittiness to the black and white picture that made Ruthie feel itchy, imagining that everything and everyone at the table was coated with matza crumbs. The twins, looking like young old women in V-necked sailor blouses and marcelled hair, stared at the camera roundfaced and grave underneath floppy hair bows.

"I thought I had a picture of them sitting at the piano, so I could show Ruthie," said Mommy, disappointed. "Doesn't she look a little like them, around the mouth . . ." Mommy made a pouty mouth for her aunts, to illustrate, and there ensued analyses of different facial features, the women tugging brows and pinching noses and contorting faces to demonstrate the Kornfeld eyelids, the Felsenbach cheekbones, the Neumann nosebridge. "Maybe there is *some* similarity," Aunt Dora finally allowed, her crackled red lips channeling smoke in Ruthie's direction. From this, Ruthie, crunching poppy seeds in her teeth, understood that she in no way resembled the astonishing twins. She took another piece of cake, disappointed that she would never play two instruments at once.

"You know, they went to Auschwitz," whispered Aunt Dora in a low serious voice. The other adults nodded and sighed, stirring their coffee, for they did know this. Then the rush of German moved beyond Ruthie, who caught only the words, "butcher" and "twins."

"Ruthie, play 'The Dreydl Song' again, with two hands," commanded Mommy, stubbing out her cigarette.

The next time Mommy's Aunt Dora went to her Golden-Ager's English class at the Jewish Community Center, she learned that her classmate Sonya Halbfinger's son Hyman was a great pianist who gave lessons. The Halbfingers invited the Kimmelmans to come to their apartment for coffee and cake that very Sunday.

But on Sunday Ruthie's sister Anna went to a birthday party, and her brother Marvin had an earache, and Daddy had to stay home with him, so Ruthie had the back seat to herself on the trip to meet the piano teacher. Her arms itched from her gold-buttoned blue coat and the pink, puffy-sleeved dress beneath it. Mommy drove, peering through the black veil that fell from her little hat, and Aunt Dora sat next to her, straightening the seams in her stockings.

"A very musical family," Aunt Dora said about the Halbfingers, her peroxided head barely showing over the back of the front seat. She spoke in German, which Ruthie understood.

"In Cologne I was acquainted with a cousin of Sonya's, Rosa Tannenbaum . . ." Aunt Dora sighed, ". . . who died in Dachau . . ." and was silent a moment. "At parties Rosa was always ready to sing *lieder* . . . Schumann, Brahms, anything any of the other guests could play."

"You see, Ruthie," Mommy broke in, raising her voice so it could be clearly heard in the back seat, "a pianist is always in demand at parties."

Mr. and Mrs. Halbfinger had matching white hair and were even smaller than old people usually were. Ruthie had to sit down in the hallway to take off her red rubber boots, and she noticed that Mrs. Halbfinger wore pink slippers with fur all the way around the top, which looked very elegant. The four adults stood in the foyer making noises of greeting and introductions, and Ruthie understood that it would be an afternoon of German and no other children.

"The little one," Mrs. Halbfinger announced, handing Mr. Halbfinger Ruthie's coat. All four adults looked expectantly at Ruthie, who felt silly on the floor and quickly stood up. She smelled a cake baking; otherwise, the air held the stuffy smell of old people's houses: talcum powder and metal radiators and windows painted shut.

"Ruth will help me hang up the coats," Mr Halbfinger announced. He grinned in Ruthie's face, exposing all his teeth and the gold clips that held some of them in place, and dumped all three coats on Ruthie's shoulder. "Come, you hold these while I take down hangers." He turned toward the closet. Ruthie staggered underneath the coats, which slipped to the floor as she struggled to hold them.

"No," she wailed. "They're too heavy! I can't carry them!" She opened her arms and let them fall into a mound of nubby wool and shiny lining.

"Coats on the floor, Ruthie!" Mommy gasped.

"I'm not big enough to hold them," Ruthie insisted with a humiliating sob. "They're too heavy! I'm too little!"

Mr. Halbfinger hitched his pants legs up his thighs and crouched in front of Ruthie, over the coats. His face looked like a skull, with its sunken eyes and protruding cheekbones.

"What is this, a big girl crying because Mr. Halbfinger asks a little help?" he demanded, smiling again. Ruthie shrunk back, alarmed by a rubbery black spot on his lower lip.

"You are too little to hold a few coats?"

"They're too heavy," Ruthie said, folding her arms in front of her. She bit her lip to keep tears inside.

"You know, Ruth, I was in a place once where children no bigger than you, children five and six years old, were able to get food to feed their entire families! They had no choice! They were big enough to jump over walls and crawl through stinking sewers. And they did it running between the legs of soldiers with guns! So how is it a big girl like you says she can't hold a few coats?" His eyes flashed with outrage.

"Stop it, Leo!" scolded Mrs. Halbfinger, picking up Mommy's coat. "What a way to talk! Leave the poor thing alone, thank God she doesn't know from such things!" Ruthie, soggy with shame at her ineptitude, looked at the floor while the trembling Mr. Halbfinger thrust a hanger into the sleeves of Aunt Dora's coat.

"Such a pretty girl," Mrs. Halbfinger said, touching Ruthie's arm, which swelled like an ugly sausage from the pinching puffy sleeve.

"What do you say, Ruthie!" Mommy prompted, poking her daughter's shoulder. Ruthie studied the moplike beige strands of carpet, hating the Halbfingers. Mrs. Halbfinger took Ruthie's hand as though they were friends, and walked with her into the living room, which was big and had windows on three sides. On the wallpaper sheep milled around beautiful blue shepherdesses with long, ruffled, low-cut dresses, and curls stacked tall like Mommy sometimes wore for fancy parties, making people say she looked like Sophia Loren who was a movie star.

The living room was filled with wonderful things, like a museum: big furniture, carved and scalloped and ruffled and strewn with web-like doilies and embroidered pillows, and lamps that were ladies with ruffled shades for hats, and ashtrays and framed pictures and figurines and cigarette servers of china and brass and glass and enamel. Ruthie wanted to examine these things, particularly the shepherdesses, but Mrs. Halbfinger tugged her through a darkened dining room. Over her shoulder Ruthie saw the adults choosing seats from a velvet and brocade array of sofas and chairs, while she was banished for failing to hold the coats. Again tears stuffed her throat. She was pulled under a cascading chandelier and into the kitchen, a narrow place papered to look as if it had red brick walls springing ivy. Here, the cake-baking smell wafted like sheets on a clothesline, filling the air so there was no talcum powder smell at all.

Mrs. Halbfinger went to a small wood table with its sides hanging down and pulled out a leather-like chair with chrome legs. "For you, I haff something very special," she said, speaking English for Ruthie. Her voice chittered like a record played at high speed. Ruthie sat down and waited to be fed.

"I said to myself," continued Mrs. Halbfinger, looking down into Ruthie's face, "is coming today a very special guest, and I must haff for her something very special. Because I haff not all the time little girls coming to my house, ja?"

This was a question, so Ruthie nodded her head, wishing the old woman wouldn't stand so close. Mrs. Halbfinger had a pretty, nearly unlined face, with thin eyebrows whose ends curved up like fish tails.

"So I said to myself, 'What does a little girl like?' And you know, once, a long time ago, I was too a little girl. You believe that?" she asked Ruthie. She laughed, a thin clucking sound that made Ruthie feel sad.

"You believe old Mrs. Halbfinger was once a little girl?"

"Yes," said Ruthie, "I know you were." Old people, Ruthie found, often asked this question, as if they were uncertain of the answer. "I know all about it," she assured the old woman. Surely Mrs. Halbfinger had been one of the little girls like Aunt Dora and Oma Sara and other aunts shut away in the photo albums: dark-haired, big-eyed girls with sausage curls, bundled into fur-trimmed coats or long-sleeved pinafores; little girls who wore dark lace-up boots, even in the summer; little girls who had refused to say "cheese" for the photographer, as if they knew that something awful was about to happen. Ruthie had been told, many times, that these little girls had lost their homes and their toys and even their families, that they had gone without food and gotten sick and even died. No one had explained to Ruthie just how they had died. ("Shh! Enough!" someone would warn. "Don't frighten the young ones! They should never know of such evil!") Ruthie gleaned that some had died from not having doctors when they were sick, and some were shot, and some were buried alive in enormous pits, and some were burned in ovens. Some of the little girls had not died in the war, and those had been transformed at once into old ladies who spoke with accents and wore sweaters and black shoes with thick heels, and who felt sad and happy at the same time when they saw new Jewish children like Ruthie. "I know you were a little girl once," Ruthie repeated.

"Then you haff good imagination," Mrs. Halbfinger replied. Standing on her tiptoes, she opened a green metal cabinet and took out a flat wrapped package which she handed to Ruthie, who trembled with fury as she unwrapped it to find that she had guessed correctly: eight crayons! A miserly box of eight, fat ones, the kind that babies used! Ruthie forced a big smile and said, "Oh, thank you, just what I wanted," in a high voice that surely sounded grown-up and fooled Mrs. Halbfinger, who might tell Mommy what nice manners Ruthie had.

Lined paper, the kind Mommy used for writing letters to Europe, appeared from a drawer. Defeated, Ruthie sat down. Mrs. Halbfinger bent over and stuck her head almost inside the oven. "So you see I know what a little girl likes!" she announced. "Now, you make a nice picture for me, and one for Mr. Halbfinger, and ven you finish, ve vill haff cake!" Without potholders, she slid the flat cake pan out, setting it to cool on top of the green stove.

She left the kitchen. Now that the cake, a long, brown roll, was out of the oven, it no longer smelled nice. Now it sent a black scratchy smell into Ruthie's throat, like when Mommy left Marvin's bottles to sterilize too long and the nipples melted. Ruthie again heard Mommy laughing, and the others joining in as if Mommy were conducting a laughter chorus. Ruthie was chained to the chair until she produced some pictures. She rocked the scratched wooden table by dancing her elbow over it, hating the fat dry crayons and the flimsy lined paper. She decided to draw a princess, because Mrs. Halbfinger, who lined her walls with frilly shepherdesses, would be impressed with Ruthie's skill at flounces and feathers. The first line veered off course when the crayon passed over a gouge in the table. Very far away, Mommy was telling a story, with Mr. Halbfinger's help ("Ja," he agreed; "ah!" he exclaimed; "sagen Sie nicht!" he marvelled, every few sentences.) Dishes clattered as everyone started laughing again. Ruthie had been forgotten.

Ruthie tiptoed back through the dining room and hid behind the arched doorway to the living room, where the adults sat among the fringe and the bric-a-brac, smoking cigarettes and sipping from tiny blue glasses that looked like thimbles. A matching blue bottle with a stopper sat by a voluptuous box of chocolates whose plundered ruffled cups spilled onto the coffee table. A man, not Mr. Halbfinger but someone taller, with black hair, rose to refill Mommy's little blue glass.

"Oh, no!" she wailed, leaning her rosy forehead into her hand. "My head is spinning already! One drop and I'm ready to make a fool of myself!"

"You could never do that," said the man, in a strange way that reminded Ruthie of herself trying to sound adult. He had black glasses that slid a little way down his long nose, and his collar stood away from his neck all the way around, even though he wore a tie.

"I will bring some cake and coffee, Mrs. Kimmelman, ziss vill help your head," said Mrs. Halbfinger, and Ruthie realized that she spoke in English. The man, who must be the piano teacher, did not have a European accent, although his words came honking through his nose, as if he had a cold.

Mommy saw her peeking around the arched doorway and patted the brocaded sofa next to where she sat so Ruthie knew it would be all right for her to join the others now. "She did not like my present," Mrs. Halbfinger said mournfully, departing for the kitchen. Ruthie called after her that she did so like it, but saying this without enthusiasm because she was afraid that she would be returned to the compulsory coloring in the kitchen. Aunt Dora came to the rescue by saying that Ruthie was eager to meet Hyman Halbfinger, her piano teacher. Hyman Halbfinger shook Ruthie's hand, which made her happy, because many adults preferred to pinch her cheek when they met her. "So you're the little pianist," he said, flashing a crosshatch of teeth rimmed by an alarming black at the gums. Pulling her hand away, Ruthie decided to like him.

"Oh, Hyman, would you play something for us?" Mommy said, and Mr. Halb-finger, who stood behind the sofa where Mommy sat, said, "Ja, ja! My boy is a wonderful pianist!" and Ruthie laughed because Hyman Halbfinger had been called a boy. A black upright piano was tucked into a corner of the room, and as Hyman Halbfinger walked toward it, Ruthie saw that on his paddle-like feet he wore brown plaid slippers with fur around the top, which looked silly with his suit. Ruthie couldn't stop from giggling because she knew that Mrs. Halbfinger had made her son Hyman wear slippers in the house, just as she and Anna and Marvin had to wear slippers in the house, because the mothers were worried that you would get a bladder infection if you walked on the cold floor in just your socks.

Hyman Halbfinger pulled a stool from under the piano and stepped over it, flipping away the back of his jacket before he sat, as if it were a tuxedo with long tails. His hands arched high, poised for attack, and then swooped down on the keys, his fingers running up and down the keyboard. Yet for all the frantic speed, his arms remained calm, while his fingers struck out in kaleidoscoping patterns, producing music so grand and fantastic that Ruthie was reminded of Liberace, whom she had seen once on "The Ed Sullivan Show," and who remained in her mind as a glorious personage. Still, Hyman Halbfinger, with his sharp nose and flipping elbows and greased strands of hair that dangled from the crown of his head which was bent low over the keyboard, did not attain Liberace's beauty and elegance.

When the piece came to a crashing, trembling, ten-fingered finish, Mr. Halb-finger leaped into the air and shouted "Bravo!" and Mommy and Aunt Dora clapped wildly in their seats and Mrs. Halbfinger stood in the doorway of the dining room clutching a silver tray of coffee and cake and looking as if she might cry. Hyman Halbfinger spun around on the stool to face his audience and nodded modestly, throwing up his hands in front of his face as if he were simultaneously displaying instruments and fending off blows.

"Do you perform?" Mommy asked, and Ruthie held her breath, because she was in the same room with a person who was about to announce an impending appearance on "The Ed Sullivan Show." But he only shook his head, and Mrs. Halb-finger said something that Ruthie didn't quite understand: Hyman had almost performed or might still perform or didn't like to perform—Hyman interjected that he loved to teach and also to play before friends, nodding as he spoke so that he appeared skinny and weak and Ruthie understood that he wasn't good enough to perform.

For some reason, Ruthie thought of the hollow-eyed five-year-old children in ragged, oversized coats, who had fed their families during the War; at the same time she had the thought that she would never be able to play piano as well as Hyman Halbfinger. These thoughts puffed through her head, filling up her eyes and nose and ears and making her shiver, although the room was so warm that the windows had steamed over above the hissing radiators that stood like silver accordions on either side of the room.

"Ruthie!" Mommy scolded, slapping her arm, astonishing Ruthie with the discovery that Mrs. Halbfinger was holding a plate nearly under her nose, and that the burned sugary smell from the kitchen was back, invading her nose from the plate, and she had to yank her head away from the plate before she got sick— ". . . a nice strudel, Ruthie, take it," someone said, but she quick covered her face with her hands to shut off the bad smell, and to not see the disgusting sticky crust, flaking away like burned skin, its insides filled with sour burned apples and bitter raisins.

". . . a beautiful strudel, Ruthie, Mrs. Halbfinger is famous for her strudel . . ."

"Nothankyou," Ruthie muttered, ready to cry because she was very, very, hungry although she was prepared to starve, until her cheeks sunk in and her ribs stuck out, rather than eat a nasty thing like that.

"If you're not hungry," said Aunt Dora, "why don't you play your song for us?" Ruthie looked down to see if her stomach had shrivelled away, but it still rested on her lap in pink-covered folds. Reverting to German, Aunt Dora announced, "The little one taught herself to play with both hands," although it was not possible that the Halbfingers had forgotten this important fact about Ruthie.

"Play," "Yes, of course, play," "Play for us!" "Play, Ruthie!" chimed the adults, so intensely eager to hear her play that Ruthie was certain that they expected music more ornate than "The Farmer in the Dell." Ruthie stood up. "I'll do it," she said, looking at no one and making a show of wiping her hands on her pink dress. She was eager to disappoint the Halbfingers, with their vinegary strudel and fat crayons and awkward son who wasn't as good a pianist as Liberace.

Ruthie sat on the piano stool for a moment at eye-level with the keys. Then Hyman Halbfinger told her to hang on and began to spin the stool with Ruthie still on it, around and around so fast that Ruthie got a good feeling again, and the way Hyman Halbfinger called out "Whee, weee," was so silly that by the time the stool arrived at the right height Ruthie felt happy and at once began to play the "Farmer in the Dell," with one finger on her right hand and three fingers on her left, and it seemed that no one was listening because she heard coffee being poured behind her and Mommy whispering. Then the song was over, and Ruthie heard Mr. Halbfinger say "Aha!" and her ears prepared for the thunder of applause, and she was about to swirl around on the stool as Hyman Halbfinger had done, about to nod her head modestly and even raise her hands as if she could bear no more praise. But before she turned around she heard the clatter of cup on plate and then, like a fire engine's siren, a scream, one long note, that grew and spread, slapping at the pretty shepherdesses on the wall and echoing off their parasols, and gathering into pools in Ruthie's ears until she jumped off the raised piano stool and hid under the piano.

The backs of two wing chairs formed stage curtains through which Ruthie saw Aunt Dora, sprawled across Mommy's lap rolling her head from side to side on the brocade sofa's arm. Aunt Dora clutched at her chest, and Mommy tried to soothe her by stroking her arms. The Halbfingers crouched around the sofa in front of the coffee table offering napkins and cognac. The vignette reminded Ruthie of one of the gruesome Jesus paintings she had seen at the Art Museum, where Jesus, bearded and bloody and wearing only a diaper, stretched bony across someone's lap in front of a cave, while people in robes knelt in concern. The screaming stopped and for a moment no one moved. Dull winter light washed the scene in sepia tones, as if the frozen moment had happened long ago and was waiting to be mounted in one of Mommy's photo albums. Ruthie wondered if Aunt Dora had died, but she became distracted by a large white plume that waved near the doorway to the dining room. It turned out to be a pale, long-haired cat, elegantly departing from the commotion ("Mein herz, mein herz," Aunt Dora moaned now, clawing at her white blouse), and Ruthie was also about to leave the terrible scene and follow the cat, hoping to play with it, when she noticed an obstacle.

On the beige carpet, between Ruthie and the cat, a small dark form progressed, slowly, trailing a broken tail like an untied shoelace. It rolled and bumped along, leaving a dark trail on the rug as it went; the grey form seemed to unravel like a ball of yarn, dropping pink strings that dragged alongside until it finally heaved over to reveal hideous innards of purple and black. It was better after all to look at the scene on the sofa.

With a magician's flourish, Mommy waved a gold pill container from Aunt Dora's purse, and Mr. Halbfinger bustled by the phone, saying he would call for an ambulance although he did not pick up the receiver. Hyman Halbfinger said that he would bring water, and in his rush to the kitchen almost didn't see the mouse. Just as his slippered foot was about to crush the mangled rodent, Hyman Halbfinger glanced down, then leaped into the air and shrieked, not as loud or as long as Aunt Dora, but nearly as high-pitched.

A great commotion ensued where Mrs. Halbfinger removed the disgusting corpse with a broom and a dustpan, all the while scolding the cat, who had vanished, and apologizing to Aunt Dora and Mommy. Aunt Dora recovered, passing her hand across her forehead many times, and Mommy tried to be cheerful, and Hyman Halbfinger, so white that the bristlings on his face stood out like pencil dots, said that he would have to lie down. Mr. Halbfinger said that they must have music, and disappeared into the dining room. A few minutes later the sound of a symphony orchestra filled the apartment, but Mr. Halbfinger didn't return. Mrs. Halbfinger scrubbed the jam-like blobs that blackened the beige strands of carpet, attacking them with a rag and a liquid that smelled like what Daddy used to clean paint brushes. Aunt Dora insisted that she was well enough to work on a barely visible spot near the sofa where her coffee had fallen. "No, no," Mrs. Halbfinger said cheerfully, from where she knelt, "it is for just such reasons I am *moderne* to have beige shag carpet!"

Mommy looked around the room and found Ruthie settled comfortably under the upright. "It is time to go," she told her, as if Ruthie were in just another seat. "Please don't get up," Mommy said to Mrs. Halbfinger, who was on her hands and knees. "Ruthie and I will find Mr. Halbfinger ourselves." Mommy held out her hand to Ruthie, who came out from under the piano and felt proud to walk hand in hand with Mommy to the dining room. Aunt Dora followed, and Mrs. Halbfinger, who *had* gotten up.

Mr. Halbfinger was seated on a dining room chair turned to face the hi-fi by the kitchen doorway. Surrounded by speakers, he waved his arms in time to the music. Mommy put her finger to her lips. She and Ruthie crept forward until they were just out of range of Mr. Halbfinger's arms. His skeletal face scrunched, revealing teeth, and he brought his waving arms down, slowly, as if they were descending a staircase. As he did this the music became quieter and quieter, until Mr. Halbfinger had reduced the sound to one violin, which he did not conduct but rather seemed to watch, as if it played beside him. Suddenly, he collected himself, sat up straight and swept his arms forward so that his suitcoat bunched around his shoulders, and as he did this the entire orchestra returned at full volume. The faster Mr. Halbfinger pumped his arms, the faster and louder the orchestra played. He struck out with one arm and a drum rolled. He stabbed the air with his hand and cymbals clashed. It was wonderful to watch, but after a few minutes Mommy took Ruthie's hand and all the ladies headed for the door.

As they got into their coats, Mommy said nice things to Mrs. Halbfinger and asked her to say good-bye to the men for them. Hyman Halbfinger appeared in the hallway wearing a red silky bathrobe and his fur-trimmed slippers and said he would call Mommy to arrange for the piano lessons, and held Mommy's hand for a long time when he told her how much he had enjoyed meeting her, as if he were unaware that the bottoms of his legs were showing, like hairy centipedes. Then he turned to Ruthie and squatted before her, carefully arranging his robe to cover his legs before placing both hands on Ruthie's shoulders.

"I want to ask you something, Ruthie," he said, composing his face into a solemn mask. "Ruthie, do you want to study piano? Do you want me to teach you? I ask because even though you are five, I will expect you to work hard."

Ruthie looked back into his round, unblinking eyes, and felt afraid, because she had been reminded again that she was five, because she was not sure what Hyman Halbfinger meant by "work hard," and because the way his long nose pointed straight at her face indicated that her answer was important.

"Oh, yes," she said, feeling as if there were a plunger in her stomach squashing down her fear. She heard Mommy exhale next to her, and when she looked up Mommy's face gleamed like a new penny, and she held her body in a way that seemed like she was dancing, although she stood still.

"I do want to take piano lessons," Ruthie repeated, staring back into Hyman Halbfinger's brown eyes, which reminded her of the little girls who stared out of the old pictures in the same, unsmiling way.

"I will work very, very hard," she promised solemnly. Hyman Halbfinger stood up and tightened his robe. Then he shook her hand with one big, grown-up shake, and from the corner of her eye Ruthie saw Aunt Dora wrap her hand around Mommy's and shake it a little as if they had just won a game, and Ruthie knew this was because of the vow she had just taken. She lifted her head in the proud manner of a girl who played two instruments at the same time, or a child who eluded soldiers to carry food to his starving family. Mommy and Hyman Halbfinger each placed a hand on her head, as if she were blessed.

All these images whirled around Ruthie, who barely noticed when Mrs. Halbfinger handed her a bar of chocolate and also the crayons. She told Ruthie that she must come again to draw pictures and play more songs on the piano, and Ruthie remembered to say thank you, and that was the beginning of piano lessons.

RUTHIE'S AUDITION

Tammie Bob

Ruthie's audition for the Music Academy was already scheduled to take place one week from the day that Mr. Klankert, the principal of her elementary school, had risen from behind his desk, taken off his glasses, and sealed Ruthie's doom: "I'm afraid there can be no place in our school for erratic behavior like this." The words tumbled like the blade of a guillotine, disconnecting the parts of Ruthie's life. Ruthie's face turned dark in anticipation of the certain smack that didn't come; instead, Mommy leaned her own reddening cheek on her open hand. "Ruthie won't continue here," she said, her voice as uninflected and sad as endless cemetery rows.

Ruthie had to leave the principal's office while he and Mommy arranged details. Would he continue yammering at Mommy about how he had never, throughout thirty-six years in the field of education, observed such an evil, organized persecution of one child by another as Ruthie had master-minded against poor Caroline Kimmelblatt? Imagine how he felt when the distraught Mrs. Kimmelblatt, tearing at her hair, brandishing her tattooed arm in his face, while shrieking at the top of her lungs that she did not survive Auschwitz for her daughter to be subjected to such indignities in America, a free country. Her daughter, tortured at the hands of children! And she reserved her vilest curses and a special spot in Hell for the ringleader, incredibly, another daughter of Survivors: Ruthie, who in the way of the Nazis had persecuted Caroline.

"Can you imagine how I felt, listening to this, Mrs. Kimmelman?" he had asked Mommy, placing his hand across his heart, a piety Mommy matched by rising and smacking her fists together in front of her chest in a gesture both defiant and saintly.

"Really, Mr. Klankert, there is some slight exaggeration here, don't you think? How dare you talk about Nazis to me! How dare you compare the affairs of children to Nazis!"

Ruthie, from a hard chair isolated in the corner of his office, saw again the black-topped playground with its random patches of slush. She felt again the cold of yesterday's icy wind spiking her face, heard again the whisper of nylon-covered legs brushing against each other as she ran, as everybody ran, across the play-ground to "get Caroline." Almost the whole class, fearless in their padded snowsuits, mittens thick like boxing gloves, had surrounded Caroline in her corner in the far part of the playground, dirty snow stained yellow and dotted with forbidding brown piles because that was where the dogs went. It was where Caroline sat at recess, and she did it because they left her alone if she sat there. If they decided she had been obedient they sometimes let her play with them the last five minutes before recess ended. But yesterday Jeffrey Hersh decided they should see what she "did" in her corner, and everyone surrounded her and Jeffrey Hersh started it: look what she "did," those turds everywhere, she always sits there and look what a mess she's made, did she pee right through her clothes or did she pull down her pants to do it? Other boys snickered, jostling each other in their excitement and echoing Jeffrey because he was the biggest and they all admired him, and the girls giggled and tried not to meet Caroline's eyes because she was looking around the circle, big scared eyes searching for an ally, a desperate smile to show that she was a good sport, that she could take a joke, as if this might yet turn into a friendly encounter or a big joke where everybody ended up laughing. Then someone threw a hard icy snowball at her, and others followed at once. A new mood surrounded the crowd, kids picking up sticks to poke her and lift her skirt, kids throwing snow and even dirt at her while she whined stop it don't, stop it don't and then screamed leave me alone just go away, and big ugly tears like snot sat on her cheeks.

Enough! Ruthie only thought it, suddenly too tired to open her mouth. Look at her friends, jumping and howling like monkeys! Look at what she had started, with those cartoons of Caroline she had drawn and passed around, enormous boobs and scribbled bush *down there*; with getting everyone to quack when Caroline walked by with her big-butt waddle; with her organized boycott of Caroline's birthday cupcakes . . . but how had those controlled meannesses resulted in this lynching? And look at Caroline, trapped crouching against the cyclone fence, waving arms and ducking her head to ward off snowballs, lifting her red, bawling face . . . it tired Ruthie to see it. She had lost her desire to punish Caroline or talk about her or think about her; why had this been so important? And why were the others tearing at Caroline so savagely . . . one boy actually flipping dog piles at her with his stick, the girls holding hands and screaming with pleasure . . . it was not them that Caroline had tried to drag into her dark, stifling life: "We have so much in common, Ruthie—Kimmelman, Kimmelblatt, almost the same . . . somewhere in Europe we might have had the same relatives." It was not with the others that Caroline had anticipated learning Yiddish or writing overseas for death certificates to document the fates of as many lost ones as possible, yet they had grabbed her hat and were tossing it back and forth over her head, spitting into it first. Ruthie looked across the playground for a teacher. Far away Mrs. Berman huddled near the entrance to the school, chatting with another teacher and not looking their way at all. It entered Ruthie's mind to get the teacher, although she knew she would never get the teacher; Mrs. Berman had already warned her about bothering Caroline. And then Jeffrey Hersh was about to kick Caroline, muddy black boot drawn back to kick her fat rear and Ruthie shouted NO! Or did she just think it? Or did someone else shout it? Jeffrey lowered his foot, hanging it near Caroline's face, and she was so utterly revolting, sobbing and hiccupping, that she wasn't like a person or even an animal that you might feel sorry for; no one could possibly take pity on something so disgusting. Jeffrey's face twisted, like it was the only way he could get his words to come out: "O.K. you goddam mutt, just lick my boots. Come on, lick everybody's boots and then you can go." She hardly argued, unable to get real words out. It was easier just to give up, to touch Jeffrey's waiting boot with her tongue and then to crawl around in the slush and put her tongue to everyone's boot. Her tongue appeared and reappeared, dropping down purple and formless, like a brain or liver or some other organ that should remain hidden. As it poked out again and again everyone got quiet. Ruthie stepped back from the circle, not wanting the dreadful tongue on her boot, shuddering as Caroline passed by. This time it was not her doing. But it didn't matter . . . whatever happened with Caroline would be forever her fault, and after all the questioning by the teacher the nurse the principal, all the calls to parents, all the finger pointing, denials, threats, it was she, Ruthie, who sat in Mr. Klankert's office the next day, while he said awful things about her to Mommy.

"Never say 'Nazis' lightly. Believe me, I suffered from the Nazis." Mommy's elegant European accent grew stronger. Her beautiful eyes brimmed with tears and she shuddered, momentarily reliving her tragedies. Ruthie's eyes watered too, as would anyone's who saw this poignant moment, even dry Mr. Klankert, who leaned forward, mouth open, and reached his arm across his desk to comfort Mommy, to take Mommy's fist or perhaps touch her waist, because he wanted to help her and save her, and because he must have fallen in love with her, as men always did. At the last moment, he caught himself, smacking his desk and tossing a dark look at Ruthie in her corner. Mommy sat down and said, "I pity Mrs. Kimmelblatt. What that poor woman went through; I can understand her seeing Nazis everywhere. We must forgive her hysteria. She is a confused soul. But we have to talk about my daughter." And then Mr. Klankert had said there was no room in school for behavior like hers, and Mommy had said she wouldn't let Ruthie stay anyhow, and now she waited outside, in the hall.

She sat on the concrete floor watching classes parade past in single file, back and forth: snowsuited kindergartners on their way to recess, sneakered fourth-graders heading for the gym, her own sixth-grade class carrying cymbals and triangles and bells and wooden blocks into the auditorium to practice the percussion concert for which Ruthie, as of now, was no longer the pianist. Now the music teacher, who lacked Ruthie's technique, would bang out "Yankee Doodle Dandy" and "You're A Grand Old Flag." As her classmates passed they peered at her, curious, as if she were a dandelion sprung through the cracked cement floor: interesting, but not worth stopping for. Pairs of her former friends began to whisper, whipping their heads around for a final look. Mrs. Berman marched by, staring directly ahead of her over the heads of her remaining students, never noticing Ruthie, who she no longer needed to know.

Mommy wouldn't tell Ruthie what she had discussed with Mr. Klankert. All her school books and an assignment sheet arrived home so that Ruthie could keep up, although all along she had been far ahead. Without gym and music and art and recess and the morning pledge and roll call, she needed no more than one hour each day for "keeping up with your class."

"These problems come from boredom, from idleness," Mommy told Aunt Dora on the phone, in German. She was spooning pieces of eggshell out of a bowl of separated whites. "In America they do nothing in school, nothing but waste time with nonsense. This is why Americans are so ignorant . . . "

Ruthie sat at the kitchen table, assigned to apple-peeling, one of several household chores designed to occupy her time that week while she waited for her audition at the Music Academy. The potato peeler wouldn't slice through the fruit's waxy skin so she flayed and gouged the apple with the peeler's rounded point, listening second-hand to Mommy speaking into the shoulder-wedged receiver, because now Mommy could scarcely bear to talk directly with Ruthie. The sound of Ruthie's voice made Mommy slump; it took most of Mommy's energy just to convey essential communications to her daughter, so that information like "Load the dishwasher," "Practice that piece again," and "I'm going out don't answer the phone," emerged in death-bed monotones.

"When a smart child gets bored she makes mischief," Mommy explained to Dora, wiping sticky shell bits off the tip of the spoon onto her hand. "First they were going to skip Ruthie ahead to the seventh grade . . . but they waited too long."

Ruthie tried again to hook the blade of the peeler under the pocked apple skin, but again it slipped off, slicing loose a flap of skin from her thumb. School had not been as idle as Mommy thought, Ruthie's only serious boredom resulting from having to memorize elemental charts and identify infinite rock samples. She pressed the flap of skin back into place, holding it until it stuck, and quickly wiped all traces of blood off the apple. "I pray she'll get into the Music Academy," Mommy said, turning away from the kitchen counter to look at her daughter. "It's her only hope."

Every night, Anna echoed Mommy's sentiments, waiting until they had switched off the light to add her thirteen-year-old's interpretation. "I'd practice if I were you," she said from her bed, right-angled foot to foot with Ruthie's. "You'll have to go to reform school if you don't pass your audition."

"I won't," Ruthie argued. "They don't have reform schools anymore. They're just trying to scare me."

"You should be scared," Anna said, arching up into a back-bridge on her squealing mattress. "In reform school they'll make you take cold showers and wear gray smocks and never let you talk. They'll take away your name and give you a number and have numbers roll call three times a day. And you better show up when they do. They have wardens who know how to smack the soles of your feet so your stomach and your liver bang together inside, but no one will believe you because it doesn't leave bruises."

Marvin kept saying it wasn't fair that Ruthie didn't have to go to school and that he wanted to stop going to school too. Mommy said that this situation was just for the week, "until the audition and then we'll see." Marvin said he'd like to audition for a Big Time Wrestling school, and Daddy, squeezing his lips together and shaking his head, said it was too bad Marvin couldn't use his big sister as an example just then, but maybe some day in the future the family could be proud of Ruthie again.

So Ruthie had no friends at home that week except when Hyman Halbfinger came to help her perfect her audition piece. They had decided that she would play Grieg's "Papillon," which flew all over the keyboard and fluttered nearly every note before it spun its lacy finish; all that finger-work impressed people although the piece itself was not that difficult to play. Once Ruthie got her fingers rolling through the patterns it almost played itself. "Magnifique!" shouted Hyman Halbfinger, in nasal French. He jumped up from the piano bench he had shared with Ruthie and applauded in the concert-goer's way, hands held high vibrating crisscross against each other. "Really, Ruthie, if you play it just like that there's no question that Mme. Edouard will accept you."

Mommy appeared in the doorway from the kitchen, looking tired and fragile, as if she needed painting and glazing and firing. "Don't swell her head," Mommy said in her new broken voice. "She needs to work harder these last few days. The last thing she needs is to think she's perfect."

Ruthie kept her face toward the piano and plucked the sheet music off the rack, pretending to peruse the paper for new insights into Grieg's "Papillon." She was afraid that if she turned around, Mommy would tell Hyman Halbfinger about Ruthie's shame. Hyman Halbfinger, who sweated easily, wiped his hand across his shiny forehead, bouncing his glass-magnified gaze from Mommy to Ruthie and back again (anyone would rather look at Mommy); he nodded his head so that his skinny neck actually touched first the front and then the back portion of his collar. Why did Mommy have to make him choose, Ruthie wondered?

"Yes, ah, of course she has to keep practicing." His voice was sad. "No question, one must always practice, practice, practice." Hyman Halbfinger, who had just be-gun a civil-service career in practical anticipation of his impending marriage (a married man needed secure benefits not available to private piano instructors), tried to smooth things with his former star pupil. "Yes, I myself live by those words, even now at the Post Office," he said to Ruthie's chubby rounded back. "If I'm at the window between customers, I practice imaginary scales on the counter. When I lift packages, I stretch my fingers as wide as I can, to keep up my finger span. When I punch figures into the adding machine, I raise my knuckles as high as they go. Even on my break, I try to take at least five minutes to do arm flexibility exercises." Ruthie snorted, thinking of the one time she had been to his parents' apartment when she was little, and old Mr. Halbfinger had conducted an entire symphony in front of the hi-fi in their dining room, leaning forward with swimming hand gestures for the slow parts while for the more dramatic sections he flung his arms so wide, so forcefully, that his suit coat threatened to split up the back. There had been no doubt in Ruthie's mind that Mr. Halbfinger had controlled the swellings and shrinkings of the symphony. Now his son Hyman Halbfinger spent his days fluttering fingers through stacks of envelopes and practicing triads on a typewriter: a sad legacy.

"Soon there'll be little Hymans running around," said Ruthie, swinging her leg across the piano bench. She smiled in a proud, sophisticated way; Mommy said nothing from the doorway and Ruthie was afraid to look and see if she thought this had been a clever comment.

"Little Hymans?" Hyman Halbfinger wondered, sweat drops gathering at the roots of his black, oily hair. "Oh—I get it! Little Hymans!" He folded his arms across his chest and tossed his head back as if he were accustomed to this topic. "Little Hymans! That's very clever, Ruthie! harharhar!" His black-rimmed teeth showed and he patted Ruthie's head.

"My goodness, Ruthie, how did you think of such a thing?" Mommy asked.

"Oh, it's very funny, very clever," giggled Hyman Halbfinger.

"Pitter patter of little feet . . ." continued Ruthie, in her new risque adult style. Actually she had first heard these things on "The Flintstones": "Soon there'll be little Freds running around," Barney had said to Fred, after Wilma had been discovered knitting booties. Ruthie had taken note, thinking that she would like to say this to someone sometime, and now she had. Hyman Halbfinger was not even married yet, but here was an opportunity for Ruthie to try out this daring line, Flintstone subtlety for the piano teacher who had, with his beaked nose and fern-like cowlicks, always reminded her of Woody Woodpecker.

"Well, Ruthie, soon you'll be pitter-pattering down the long halls of the Music Academy . . . I know it, and I do envy you. Yes, I really do," Hyman Halbfinger said in unblinking sincerity. Mommy beat him to the coat closet, handing him his coat and his new feathered fedora; already he dressed like a father. Gone were the days when he accepted coffee and cake and conversation with Mommy, the two of them laughing at frequencies that caused their cups to shake, filling the saucers with cascading coffee which Mommy staunched with napkins, which remained soaking brownly in the saucers, while Hyman Halbfinger, giggling, told Mommy of his madcap escapades in the practice rooms of the Music Academy, and Mommy encouraged him to pursue his dreams, illustrating her advice with tales of her far-flung adventures. These days, Hyman was a man with commitments; the government position, night classes in accounting, and his betrothed, the mysterious "Nancy" who had chosen Hyman Halbfinger over all the men in the world, ending forever Ruthie's years of satisfying piano instruction. "The timing is just a coincidence," Hyman Halbfinger had assured the Kimmelmans, "really, Ruthie needs to work with someone else . . . I don't think I can take her much farther. We've gotten too comfortable together. She needs to be stretched."

Ruthie's first sight of Mme. Edouard reminded her of Hyman Halbfinger's cruel words, for the very tall white-haired lady appeared to have spent considerable time on the rack. All her limbs seemed extended beyond their intended limits: her neck-scarf wrapped twice around above her starchy collar; her wrists requiring wide bangles besides her cuffed sleeves; a back that descended at such length that her narrow belt seemed designed to keep it from continuing to the floor.

"She was a famous pianist," Mommy had told Ruthie in the car on the way to the audition. Hedges of rain scratched at the car; the windshield wipers labored in worried rhythm: "Last chance, last chance," they scratched out, scaring Ruthie. "For many years she travelled the world, giving concerts and interviews," Mommy said, driving very slowly so that every other car passed them, giving the sensation of driving through a car wash. "A few years ago, her husband, a pretend duke, the last of a long line of husbands with false titles, ran off with a young Italian movie star. Mme. Edouard shut all her windows and turned on the oven . . . do you understand, Ruthie? She tried to gas herself! It was in all the newspapers."

Ruthie looked down at her sheet music, planted on her lap just so she didn't have to see the fat in her thighs spread all across the car seat. She couldn't decide whether or not to bring the music; certainly she would have to play Grieg's "Papillon" from memory, but what if Mme. Edouard wanted to refer to the score? Still, she didn't want to insult her by suggesting that she might not be familiar with such a common composition. Why had she picked something so trite, anyhow? "She only accepts prodigies," Mommy had told Aunt Dora on the phone. Ruthie knew she was not a prodigy, although if Mme. Edouard accepted her, would she become one?

Mommy switched on the radio, swerving the car. Nancy Sinatra was on, of course. "These boots are made for walking, and that's just what they'll do, and one of these days these boots are gonna walk all over you-ou-ou-ou . . ." Mommy sang as if she were alone in the car, bouncing in her seat. Her voice was much higher than Nancy Sinatra's. Ruthie tried to play "Papillon" in her head, but it was impossible with the bass going so loud. "Tee la la lee la, tee la la lee la, tee la . . ." Mommy sang, not knowing the words. There was no air in the car, none, and Mommy's singing stuck in Ruthie's nose, and her throat. "How come she didn't die?" Ruthie screamed. Mommy turned down the radio. "Who?" Mommy asked, taking a hand off the wheel to wind one of her red sideburn tendrils around her finger.

"Who?" Ruthie said. "Mme. Edouard, that's who! You said she turned on the gas and closed the windows!"

"Oh," Mommy said, as if it was no big deal. Every night she put one roller in each sidelock to preserve the perfect spiral shape. "Yes, well, I suppose you're almost old enough to understand. Her lover found her, at the last moment, when she had already fainted, and carried her outside, unconscious. All the newspapers carried the picture, a famous picture, of him, sleeves rolled up, crying over her. She was stretched out on the grass, in a white nightgown with her black hair streaming everywhere."

Ruthie didn't understand . . . if Mme. Edouard had had a lover, why did she try to kill herself over an unfaithful husband? Perhaps her lover had not been a duke or any kind of title at all. Why would a woman like that even consider Ruthie as a piano student? Ruthie wiped steam off her window and saw the gray, steamy, tree-circled lake that faced the Music Academy. She had forgotten about that terrifying lake, filled with dead bodies. A few years ago, a perfect skeleton of a mastodon had been found in the lake and reassembled in the lobby of the Music Academy. Once Daddy had taken Ruthie to see the mastodon, but the enormous bones had made her cry, fogging her eyes so that she never really saw the entire thing, only a blur of immense tusk, an infinite slope of backbone.

When Daddy took her to see the mastodon Ruthie had been little, although almost strong enough to hold Daddy from advancing, rooting her feet wide by the glass front doors of the Music Academy. "Now, you are too big to be scared of a bunch of old bones," Daddy had said, pronouncing his English precisely.

"I'm not scared," said Ruthie, quavery. Daddy pulled her hand, dragging her into the Music Academy's enormous egg-shaped lobby, where the mastodon's black eye sockets poured wrath over the people carrying black instrument cases and folders of music, people who scuttled to and from the walls of elevators, people oblivious to the monster in the lobby.

"He was alive many, many years ago, but now he and all of his kind are gone," said Daddy. "The skeleton is all that remains." Ruthie began to cry, blurring the sight of the behemoth's enormous bones, strung together by wire that anyone could see was too delicate, so at any moment the entire structure would shatter, mammoth bones that would explode a crater into the black marble floor.

"I won't see it!" Ruthie screamed, and when Daddy, embarrassed, tried to pick her up, she threw herself down on her back kicking (and she decided not to care about her underpants showing), and then a woman in a blue brimmed hat appeared and smiled at Daddy with slitty eyes and said, "It looks like a woman's touch is called for here," as if she were about to clean a shirt on TV.

She crouched down over Ruthie but smiled upward, at Daddy. "Now, now," said the woman, "we're going to behave, right now." Ruthie became quiet and rigid at the sight of this stranger hovering over her but looking at Daddy. The woman wanted to leave her with the bones and take Daddy away. The woman's lips were very red with cracks around them, and when she touched Ruthie's arm Ruthie began to scream again. Daddy picked her up and ran with her from the Music Academy, the arched tusk overhead pointing the way out. They went to see the movie "The Snow Queen" instead, but it was about a beautiful, wicked queen with slitty eyes and red lips just like the scary blue-hatted woman in the museum, so Ruthie never remembered anything about the movie except that it took place in an icy land, with lakes where frozen mastodons awaited revenge.

Now Mommy parked, pulling in and out of the space, adjusting her angle by inches each time: "It's so tight!" she complained, as if she were putting on an old skirt. "God help me, I'll never fit!" Ruthie watched the lake out of her foggy window, and for a moment a toothy human skull seemed to float on the choppy surface, bobbing in a natural, almost cheerful rhythm. There were bones in that lake, she was sure . . . about what? Something about a body, hadn't the newspapers been full of that? She had cut a picture of the mastodon out of the paper and taken it to school. The newspaper had said the mastodon was in perfect condition but rather small for any of the important natural history museums to be interested; that was why it had gone to the Music Academy. Ruthie decided not to be frightened of it today. She was too old now, but still! Just beyond those glass doors swooped the enormous tusks, and if a disaster of some sort occurred, an earthquake, for example, a dozen people might be impaled at once!

"Mommy," Ruthie said, suddenly remembering what she had forgotten, "this is the lake where the body of the boy was found, isn't it?"

"What?" said Mommy. She was unfolding a plastic rainbonnet that she got from a bowl at the beauty shop. "What boy?"

"The boy with no head," Ruthie said angrily, because Mommy knew perfectly well which boy; it was not as if boys always turned up at the bottom of this lake. "It was in the newspaper," Ruthie continued, finding herself too breathless to say more.

"Oh," said Mommy, tucking in the front of her hair. "It's been years . . . You shouldn't be thinking about that, when Mme. Edouard is waiting."

"I remember his name was Danny Margolis," Ruthie said. "He was ten years old. Did they ever find his head?"

"I don't know," Mommy said, opening the door. "You always ask such terrible questions, Ruthie! You worry about the wrong things, the wrong things impress you! It makes you . . . un-normal!"

"Do you think I would actually kill somebody?" Ruthie asked. Mr. Klankert had said it was impossible to know what someone like her was capable of doing. Maybe she was worse than she had thought. Her hands squeezed the sheet music, crumpling and shredding the edges. She should have put the music in a folder; now the rain would finish ruining it. "Do you think I would cut off somebody's head?" She had wanted to make Mommy laugh, but instead of floating lightly away her words hung in the car like oily sausages in a butcher shop.

"Who knows what you would do anymore?" said Mommy, echoing the principal. She inflated an umbrella before her and let it pull her out of the car on a gust of wind. They ran toward the building, Ruthie behind, using the sheet music to shield her head from the whirling rain, and once inside, from the sight of the dreaded roped-off centerpiece of the egg-shaped lobby. Even so, Ruthie couldn't help seeing backbones lined up like plates in a dish drainer, toe bones splayed like lightning rods.

"How honored I am to meet you," Mommy said, dipping her body just slightly in a courtly, un-American way. After a moment Mme. Edouard, forgetting to smile, extended her hose-like fingers for Mommy to kiss. She snatched them back after the briefest possible handshake but Mommy continued to smile at her, one full-blown siren acknowledging another who was retired but not forgotten. Ruthie stared rudely, fleshing this long, stretched-out woman into the glamorous pianist who filled the concert halls of Europe, the tragic subject of a famous photograph who had lain unconscious in the grass in a misty nightgown, black hair streaming, while a distraught lover wept over her in his shirtsleeves.

"I must have had a dozen calls from Halbfinger about young Ruth," said Mme. Edouard, her voice surprised, lacy and ruffled like a doily, but in all the soft frilliness it was unclear whether Mme. Edouard was pleased by Hyman Halbfinger's intercessions.

"We are greatly honored that you have taken into your esteemed consideration the possible acceptance of the training for Ruthie's continued musical studies," said Mommy, whose English suffered under stress. Ruthie shuddered, and a sideways look at Mme. Edouard revealed her long thin mouth unzipped beneath her reedy nose; she was smiling at Ruthie, pitying Ruthie for having such a preposterous mother, a puffed-up mother, with piled red hair and snappy checkerboard vinyl miniskirt. What appeared unattainably elegant and gorgeous in the eyes of most people, like Daddy and Mr. Klankert and Hyman Halbfinger and Uncle Sol and the Kleinermans and Aunt Dora and almost everyone that met Mommy, did not impress others, generally thin-lipped women like Mme. Edouard. She was like Ruthie's friend Paula's mother. ("My mother says it's shameful that your mother gardens in short shorts in the *front yard,*" Paula reported, "and especially because she has fat legs." Paula's mother always wore golf skirts appliqued with farm animals or fruits, skirts that descended to the tops of her skinny knees, which protruded like wrinkled baseballs.)

"Would you like to warm up, Ruth." ordered Mme. Edouard, crooking her neck backward toward a great black grand, shiny with grinning keys, the hugest piano Ruthie had ever seen, although somehow in her nervousness she had incredibly managed *not* to see it. Ruthie looked at it and then quickly away, as if it were too bright. The piano took up over half the space; other than a few orange plastic chairs it was the only object in the long, narrow white room, arching in front of the floor-to-ceiling window like an immense fly. Ruthie had never played a grand piano before, had never touched one or even been closer to one than the first gallery of the concert hall. "A few scales, whatever you like," Mme. Edouard warbled in her trilly voice.

Ruthie seated herself on the round three-legged stool which she scratched back and forth across the floor, unable to find the correct distance from the keyboard, which spread out across from Ruthie's shoulders. She rose to spread the music to Grieg's "Papillon" on the piano's music stand, but the wadded, crackled paper wouldn't stand.

"I don't need music," Ruthie called out in an untruthful voice, and when she turned to somehow dispose of the music there was Mommy, hand outstretched.

"I think we can raise the stool, don't you?" said Mommy, quickly glancing back at the erect Mme. Edouard before turning the round stool, first slowly, hand over hand, until the brown disc seemed to spin itself in a blurry whir, dancing like a top. This made Ruthie want to ride on the stool, as she had done the first time she met Hyman Halbfinger at his parent's apartment, when she had been five years old. There had been many German-speaking grownups in the room waiting to hear her play songs she had taught herself on the piano, and Ruthie, who was hungry, had felt angry. Hyman Halbfinger had spun her on the stool, shouting "whee-whee!" in a very silly way, which made the room spin and Ruthie laugh. After whirling around it had become easy to play the songs, and everybody applauded.

Mommy finished spinning the stool and backed away toward Mme. Edouard, holding the crumpled music in two fingers like a used tissue. Ruthie sat down again, now higher above the keyboard than she needed to be, but she stayed on the stool and began a C-scale. The notes sprang out, running together like spilled paint, and in the loud confusion Ruthie lost track of her fingers.

"Don't you practice your scales, Ruth?" asked Mme. Edouard's voice. Ruthie looked across the piano at the tall window, where Mme. Edouard's haloed outline dripped down the glass among the raindrops.

"I've never played a grand piano before," Ruthie said to the window. "I didn't know it would be so—loud. The notes came out so fast. The grand piano surprised me."

"We have a very fine piano," Mommy said. Her outline did not appear in the window. "Not a grand, but it has an excellent tone. Ruthie has played many different pianos with no difficulty."

"I'm sure we're a little nervous then?" said Mme. Edouard impatiently. "Just try to ignore it."

Ruthie's hands dove into some Czerny exercise that it turned out she didn't exactly remember—the truth was that Ruthie rarely practiced scales or fingers exercises the way a pianist was supposed to; she only practiced pieces that she liked. Hyman Halbfinger used to whine about this: "Ruthie, you'll never develop style if you don't have a strong foundation of technique . . . twenty minutes of scales every day—minimum!" The sweat of righteous conviction would dot his hairline while Ruthie stubbornly slumped over the keyboard. Eventually he gave up and stopped assigning the boring exercises and variations, and it seemed Ruthie had developed a style anyhow, for on occasion Hyman Halbfinger had been overheard saying that when Ruthie mastered a piece her interpretations were outstanding. But Mme. Edouard would expect her to practice scales, Ruthie could tell.

Mommy coughed, which reminded Ruthie that she somehow had to erase the silence in the room. Ruthie twaddled her fingers over the keyboard; miraculously, the opening runs of Grieg's "Papillon" emerged. Instead of a weightless butterfly blown through the air, shards of glass seemed to pour out of the grand piano in the same way that hard raindrops outside pelted the long window of the Music Academy. Ruthie sprayed icy rivers of notes at Mommy and Mme. Edouard, who stood at the back of the long room watching Halbfinger's chubby protégé waggle her stumpy arms up and down the keyboard, unwittingly reinterpreting Grieg's little ditty, without much technical competence yet with an energy, a bravado, that was sometimes near brilliance and other times overreaching and pathetic. What could the child mean by trying to vibrate the keys during the series of *glissandos*? Overall, her effort was admirable, sometimes even inspired. Mme. Edouard reflected briefly on that overdone business about technique being teachable, where artistry was not. This aphorism seemed overrated, most often quoted by those who lacked both. And why not accept the girl? What did she really care, anymore?

Mme. Edouard glanced beside her at Mrs. Kimmelman who was winding the much folded sheet music around her fingers and watching Mme. Edouard out of the side of her painted, heavy-lidded eyes. Mommy caught Madame's pouched, sagging glance and gazed back, nodding as if she were accepting congratulations on Ruthie's behalf. Mme. Edouard turned quickly away, thinking that so many of the students at the Music Academy were the children of camp survivors . . . there were hordes of them, pounding pianos and sawing violins and blowing flutes . . . surely Mrs. Kimmelman was a camp survivor, the accent, the false humility, the way she twisted that pathetic shred of paper as if she would do the same with her daughter's neck if she failed this audition.

The piece concluded with a low note, staccato, and Ruthie bounced her left hand off the note and for some reason whacked the ledge of the noble grand piano. Mommy laughed. "Nice, nice," said Mme. Edouard, softly. Ruthie swiveled around on the stool to face her. She was afraid to look at Mommy.

"How do you think you played that?" asked Mme. Edouard. She had not once moved from the spot near the back wall where she had stood since Ruthie and Mommy had entered the room.

"All right, I guess," Ruthie answered, hating her.

"You guess? Surely you must know?"

"I thought it was good," The words became false as soon as she said them. She fidgeted, sliding one hefty thigh and then the other off and then back on the side of the stool.

"And why did you think it was 'good'?"

Ruthie had no answer to this. Others were supposed to critique her playing, not her. Now she looked at Mommy who offered no protection at all.

"It was good because I didn't make any mistakes."

"And besides that? Were you thinking about the notes? Were you thinking about Grieg, or about *le papillon*?"

"No."

"No? None of those things? Then maybe you were worried about whether I would accept you into the Music Academy?" Mme. Edouard advanced until she towered in front of Ruthie, a giant stalk of celery trying to dip into her vanished thoughts. Mommy opened her purse and dropped the music inside, preparing to leave, as it was clear that Ruthie was offending Mme. Edouard, her last hope, although Mommy planned to report that Ruthie had played more brilliantly than she had ever heard her play.

"Ruthie has been very excited about the idea of coming to the Music Academy," Mommy said, to Mme. Edouard's back. "I'm sure that's what she was thinking about."

"No! I wasn't!" Ruthie cried. "Actually, I was thinking about the boy who was killed . . . Danny Margolis!"

"Oh, my," said Mme. Edouard, putting her banana-like hand to her jaw.

"Because I could see the lake from the piano, you see, right out the window," jabbered Ruthie, and turned and pointed, and Mme. Edouard leaned forward to look and Mommy came over to the piano to look too, out the rainy window at the dark gray sky that sank down to the green-gray lake surrounded by blowy, leafless trees.

"They found his body in the lake," Ruthie continued, "and they never found his head. And I was thinking—that maybe his head is still there. He was collecting his paper route money one night and he never came back, and then a long time later they found his body in the lake without the head." Ruthie gasped a little. "They never found who killed him, but they think his head was cut off with hedge clippers!"

"Stop it, Ruthie!" Mommy ordered. "She has a terrible mind," Mommy explained, sure that Ruthie's outburst had destroyed any chance that she might be accepted. Mme. Edouard leaned backward, away from Mommy. "It's not so bad," Madame said. "It's imagination, I think. Your daughter is a sensitive one, isn't she?"

"Sensitive! She's always imagining the worst cruelties. I don't know from where she gets it."

"So would you like to begin at the Academy on Monday?" Mme. Edouard asked Ruthie. Ruthie looked down at her spread-out lap, and hooked her feet around the tripod base of the stool. Mommy laughed.

"Just like that? Well, she plays very well, doesn't she?" she demanded of Mme. Edouard, her equal once more. "Oh, my. Of course she wants to come! It is a great honor to us that she has passed your high judgment!"

And so it was arranged, the next hour being spent following Mommy from one office to the next, filling out forms, having a tour of the building ("You are assigned practice times but you may sign up for more if your other grades are all 'B's or higher," said the headmaster, which was what they called the principal. "We expect the highest academic performance from our young musicians.") "We are so excited, such an opportunity . . ." Mommy kept saying to each person that they met. "The most wonderful honor . . . I only hope she can appreciate . . ." But Ruthie barely heard a word anyone said, didn't memorize the locations of her classrooms or the names of her teachers. I wish I was brave enough to run away, she thought, in books sometimes kids run away and it works out all right, but I could never do it.

"I don't think I know enough music to be in the Music Academy," she confided to Mommy in the car going home. Now there was opera on the radio and Mommy sang the aria from "Madame Butterfly" with tragic exuberance although she could not reach many of the notes. "I don't know why I was accepted."

"So you'll learn!" Mommy sang. "That's what you're going for! Things always work out for the best, you can see for yourself how true that is . . . from such a bad situation to such great honors, Ruthie! I only hope this time you appreciate good fortune . . ."

IN PURE SOFTNESS

Polly Mills

The split-levels, A-frames, and brick bungies were puny, poking through burned, muddy yards in the Midwestern plain, cowering under their low, sloping roofs. How absurd were these guardians of Bardy Tenngren's limitless childhood memory. The blue painted bottoms of Lombard Commons pools flashed across the train's window in a heartbeat, not in the breadth of those many summers. And although he'd been inside each house in the next four blocks, one went by faster than the others, snatching at him, the one he and Mom had painted avocado green.

It wasn't until they stood on the sidewalk before this house, under Allison's lollipop tree (its neglected branches now bowed over the brown lawn), that Bard saw that the ruffled yellow curtains in the kitchen windows had been replaced by wooden shades. Someone's rusted black Datsun started up in the driveway. The face inside that car robbed Bard's comprehension—it was a stranger's.

"Where are we going, Bard? You know that kid?"

He didn't answer.

"How come we're just standing here?"

"Don't know."

The train had warmed her up, and Bard's spitty kisses. But Melissa was tired, and she felt really old. Hardly ever had she felt this kind of fatigue, as if it were reaching way down into her and stealing parts that she had always relied on—her tough-talking resilience—and parts she had been saving—maybe wisdom—for better times. Yeah, she was almost empty, and she almost cried. Because she didn't feel like a kid anymore. No fucking way.

"We're going to the Commons," Bard said. "I gotta show you something." Because his house was closed to him. Home. He couldn't go up there, knock, and get back into his old room, find his microscope, the Snoopy rug, or jack shit.

He would take the meandering route, past Timmy Bresler's house, a stained, stucco facade—and at the house that had been his foster home, he'd look for Allie's rusted blue bike in the yard.

But Lombard had shrunk. How could the houses have ever been this low? He felt that, if he craned, he could see over the tops of them, his eyes lighting on the tar-papered old roofs, and find—once and for all (his mother would thank him) the squirrels' nests clogging the gutters.

Perhaps the winter had burned the soppy grass brown, but deeply, illogically, he was sure it had been his prolonged absence that had drained the green, the perfume, the adventure—a keenly-known, daily, tasted, smelled, fingered, spoken, overheard, seen, and PLAYED lust for life from the place . . . HIS voice, his yelping, high notes sailing up into the trees. Yeah, Bardy's boyhood was what the village had learned, bitterly, to live without. But who was laughing? This insight only made Bard sorry—for himself, but, no, for everyone.

Only Melissa, for sure, had a note of fresh life in her. In a rotting world, frozen, melting in the sun in the cold air, her eyes burrowed deeply into him, hoping.

"My childhood sucked," he told her, summing it up with a courage his hindsight rarely allowed him. "My mom used to beat the shit out of us." And he could have gone on and on, but his body—its bones and muscles grown long and strong—forbade it. His body, its iron shell, would not allow the felt details of throbbing bruises, cuts and welts, hard strikes that burned his skin and muscles and rattled his head, bones, his center of balance, until he'd had to hunker down into a squat, and from the floor of his closet, then, throw out—and up at her—his weakling's bites and kicks.

Melissa's eyes traveled his chest and broad shoulders until they settled on the soft spot between his pecs, where he'd been hiding everything. "You love me, don't you, Bard?" but he wished she hadn't said it. He grabbed her hand, and they tore off walking.

Once, with Allie, this soft feeling in him almost came when he had crawled from the roof, in through his bedroom window, through the hole in the *shoji* screen. And it had been a throbbing, humid, black summer's night. And he'd been stoned. And Allie, a Buddha with long, shimmery hair, sat up on his bed in the blue dark.

He'd been out past curfew, but she hadn't said a word. Fifteen, feeling absurd, he had crawled up beside her, and absurder, he had pulled off his shirt. Then his back felt the good itch of the burlap on his wall, and he'd rubbed himself—to burning—into it. And the side of his arm felt a quieter shock of warmth and softness—Allie—her hot arm. And they had sat like that for a long, rare time.

They smelled Dad, his ferment, roll over in his sheets in the living room behind them. Dad's snores curled, spiralled, filling the space between them and his couch. Through the long rip in the *shoji* screen, under five white stars, Mom's yellow window glowed. For she lived across the alley.

And then they were a family. And the heat, sticky, smelling sweetly of brown bananas in the kitchen, seeped into him. And he was surrounded by love, an absurdity. And NEVER before had he, so softly, understood the sadness.

He'd whispered to Allie, while they both stared keenly ahead, "Nobody loves me. I'm crazy. I might die. And there's nobody I can talk to."

And Allie, her heat, shining (she was his sister Buddha), only held him there—rooted—by a thin strip of hot skin—her arm pressed into his.

No, Bard thought now, squeezing her hand, Lissa was a different person, and probably better. Because she was one of the kids who had grown up in pure softness of strokes and burrowing cuddles with no fear or tricks behind them. When a kiss was a kiss on the top of the head, and nobody would change their mind, pull back, and reel you a mind-boggling blow. Because Lissa was virgin to such insult, and her body, soft, in black, a mind-boggling infinity of deep crannies and curves, had played and laughed and played.

"I'm glad nobody ever hurt you," he said, when the brown tree branches hung down, an arch, over the sidewalk, and a line of red brick two-stories insulted his soft spot—the way he remembered.

"No, nobody ever hurt me," she admitted. "That's the beauty of being invisible, of being able to go unnoticed by your parents, by your whole family. They don't touch you when they can't tell if you're there."

He admired her. The slanted afternoon sun cut his eyes, and reflected in gold specks in the backs of her pupils. Yeah, better than sunlight, her light (tricky, for it lay under darkness) was reliable. Hardly anyone knew it, but Bard saw Melissa's sheer brilliance.

"You're fucking smart," he said.

"I know."

"So am I—it's my main attribute."

"Yeah, you told me. You're a genius—" but she was sarcastic.

"Not everybody makes it," Bard said, honestly. "Some kids are too dumb—or weak—or cowards."

"I sort of feel like a coward, these days," she told Bard.

"But don't. Because you're not."

She stared simply back at him.

It was just about the most honest talking he'd ever done with a girl, and he felt it burning him. His face burned, and he had to piss a hard, rusted, hot stream, and now what could she do to him? He'd let down his guard. Not just the sadness, making him tell stuff, but his body felt soft, mushy, and weak.

They were at the edge of the Commons Park now, heading into a playground.

He tore away from her and crash-landed on the merry-go-round. "Push me!" he demanded, his back, through his army jacket, feeling, remembering the steel V pattern of quilted metal treads in the platform.

"No."

"I'm pushing myself!" He crawled on his back until one long leg dangled over the edge and felt solid ground. Then he scraped, his foot taking flying leaps, as the sky spun—china blue, but gray-edged where feathers of cirrus clouds spun apart from each other toward the edges of Bard's field of vision. This was centrifugal force, and he was immune in its center.

"Jump on!" he shouted, but from the corner of his eye, at each go-round, he saw a new, smaller, blacker Melissa. An upside-down triangle. Her hands shoved deeply into her pockets, shoulders hunched, head down, she was taking giant steps backward—away from him.

"LISS-AAAA!" he howled. "LISS—A—A—A—A—A—A," as the platform of the merry-go-round vibrated under him, the screw loose.

His shining, bright, strong-voiced A's, "A—A—A—A—A—A—A—A!" soared out and over Lombard, Shithole, Illinois, until the housepets in each house facing the park howled, and an Army chopper, surveying the Midwest, swirled close, then dipped down, and the whole village—Bardy felt it—succumbed to the spinning, centrifugal pull of Bard, captain of all destiny. For . . . once again his high notes rattled their windowpanes, and they would, every fucking last one of them, lean into him, SEE something, and remember.

He scooted back until his head hung over the edge of the merry-go-round and he felt the dirt and sometimes mud roused by his hair. And the scene: bald trees; broken sidewalk leading back into a dense, narrow row of front yards; the slide; and Melissa, repeated itself each time he spun past it—a round rhythm, with the black, riveting image of Melissa as a downbeat that thrumbed, that faded. With each spin, she backed away.

He let his head clunk the ground—a thousand clunks—who cared if it fucking killed him? For he would like to die like this, surrounded by memory, by the last place where he had been sure he was alive. And it wouldn't be bad at all to spill out for good, holding Lissa in the corner of his eye.

"Bardy, stop it," she hollered, her voice steady. And she rushed up. And the bars of the merry-go-round handles slammed twice into her thighs before Bard's head hit her legs, which would not be moved. And he sat up, laughing, then turned his back to her, over the edge of the go-round, and puked.

Then she would have walked away from him. Because, Bard, there was something really, really wrong. Except how the hell had she even gotten to this place? And even with eighteen dollars, how exactly would she get back?

Bard pulled himself off the merry-go-round and headed, like HE knew where he was going, deeper into the sprawling park.

And the khaki back of Bard's jacket, almost camouflaged to any but a most searching eye in the surrounding greens and grays and browns, DAMN him, watched her. And it was that patch of khaki and the muddy, blond back of Bard's head, and his long legs in jeans, and the black, shiny army boots striding faster and faster away from her, that she knew was her only, crazy chance.

"Bardy! Wait up!" she called, and cut into a run, but her thighs, hit hard by the bars of the merry-go-round, nearly buckled under her. "Fuck you, Bard," she cried.

He turned around, tipped his head up to the sky, and stood still until she ran up to him.

She punched him, all knuckles, in his soft spot, and he grabbed himself there, feeling it. "Yeah, I love you, Lis," he confessed, his voice raspy.

"So what?" she said.

He wrapped his arm around her waist.

"You smell like vomit." She pulled away from him and walked, parallel with his broad strides, ten feet away.

"I love Lissa Jensen!" he roared to the whole fucking town.

And she scowled grandly.

The boy's bathroom in the fieldhouse smelled exactly the same, reeferonderful.

Probably his graffiti was long gone, but somebody else kept the flame. And now some punks had scrawled "Impeach Nixon" on the door to one of the shitholes, a concept beyond his time. Bard scowled. Today's youth was going down the drain. He pictured kids in kindergarten today, coming in here to whiz in ten years, tall, round-headed assholes, in a future that outscoped Bard, to draw graffiti about faggots, he figured, in cars that flew.

His hot piss streaked ochre into the porcelain urinal; he aimed it up broadly across the wall.

Melissa came in and caught him tucking in his dick. He smiled. She bent over the middle sink to drink, and then he saw—full view—her boney ass. It was not what most guys would consider an attribute, but it was, to Bard, at that moment, shamelessly beautiful. He came up beside her and drank also from the faucet, then washed his face and the inside of his mouth with pink, runny soap, searching out puke remnants with his index finger. He spat. He washed his neck and hands. He dunked his head under the shocking, cold, running water, and told her, "Melissa, Lissy, Lissa, will you wash my hair?"

And when he felt her warm ten fingers rubbing his head—his wagging crown and his aching temples—and the pink soap ran, stingingly, into the cut on his eye, he felt nearly as smart, as brilliant, as Melissa. Because, God, what was this? Something sexy he had never felt—dreamed of—before. "LISSa," he moaned at her.

Because, no, she thought, Bardy was not crazy. He was brave. And crazy was the greatest thing. Maybe he was sick, sad, inside, but show her one kid she knew who wasn't. It was this sadness that tore at her. It was crazy, but she tore off her jeans jacket, arguing with herself that the cuffs were drenched. Then her sweatshirt and blouse. And . . . crazy felt like knowing exactly what she was doing, for once, for a change.

She rubbed the back of his neck, and Bardy whimpered. She peeled off his coat and shirt. He turned around; he tucked his cold, wet hands under her bra, and cupped her breasts.

"Somebody could walk in," she said.

"Who?"

"I don't know. This is your home town."

"Take off your pants . . . and underpants. I'm gonna wash YOUR hair."

"You're nuts, Bard."

But she did, and he soaped her, and his hand roamed. And Melissa was the smartest girl the world had ever known. She felt her body's wisdom and it glowed. "Put your fingers inside, Bard," she whispered, but intent, he didn't hear. His finger . . .

"Man, Melissa." She was soft, hot, slippery, incredible inside.

"The mayor," he murmured, his words, floating, out of time.

"Huh?" She could laugh, she could laugh right now, because this felt, kind of, like serious tickling.

"That's who could come in."

Her hips leaned, knowingly, into his hand, "Or . . . probably one of your long-lost relatives."

"I don't have any," he laughed, "I'm an orphan."

And, no, it wouldn't, it couldn't be like this, not in the piss-smelling john. And Bard remembered his plan, but it, a child's funny memory, could not encompass his feeling. He had French-kissed eight girls, and felt tits, a total of five. And one time, when someone's slutty so-called sister had visited at St. Charles, everyone had gotten a chance, for fifteen hard-to-come-by bucks, to rub her, through panties, under a math book, under a lunch table, from the outside.

He gently pulled Melissa, his finger inside, up against the sink, and rinsed her, splashing the cold water across her hips and legs. Then with a million paper towels —cascades of paper towels—they sort of dried one another off.

"I know exactly where to go," he said, his eyes shining. "I've been saving it."

They dressed.

He led her out of the bathroom, and the Orphanage stood up green ahead of them. "See that?" He pointed to a tall clump of evergreens in the center of the wet field.

"What?"

"THAT." He knew it would be O.K. inside.

"Those bushes?"

"The Orphanage."

"What?"

"Me and Allie used to come here. You've got to see it inside." And on the inside, something, he could see it, great would happen. Not just the floating Bard would be there, but somebody else, someone little and good, who he sweetly dared to remember.

They crawled through a bald spot between two trunks and followed a narrow path under heavy, acrid boughs.

"Perfect," she said, the pine smell making her wise.

The snow hadn't been there. In the hollow center of the thick stand, the ground was dry, worn to a sheen. He even imagined that it was warmer inside. "This is the auditorium, where they bring kids to pick out better parents," Bard said, his voice small and strong. And then two Bardys were talking; Melissa heard the resonance. "Your real parents don't have to be dead for you to come here; you just have to be sick of the ones you've got."

"No problem, Bard."

He led her over the fallen trunk, shiny as a bench seat, just as he'd remembered, and they sat down. The needles dipped lower here, and the light was nearly obscured —a gray green. "This was my room. Private," he whispered. "Once, Allison and her friend Karen tried to come in here, so I whizzed on them."

"Charming."

"I was only seven."

"Were you cute when you were seven?" But she knew he was; she could see it, right now, all over him.

"I was a pisser."

"So nothing's changed."

"Naw."

And this kissing was definitely different, because Bard, a virus-riddled boy, who had never smelled a day clear of snot, breathed free. Or he didn't breath at all. Or he breathed in every inch of Melissa. They fell back off the log and onto the dry, shiny ground. And next he would taste her. And finger her—every nub and curve. And his voice, quite small, moaned.

"You love me, don't you, Bardy," she cooed at him, as she struggled up onto her knees. And he, reaching up from the ground, unpeeled her and unpeeled himself, her smart hands guiding his every move.

"This is not love," he heard himself say, but without mere words. His hands and arms and shoulders, his mouth, his yearning hips, tried very hard to pull her down toward him, to explain to her—this incredible body, this Melissa—how love was touching, and not an absurdity of feeling, and not words. And she would never trick him, slap, or switch, or beat him. Because the entire point of everything was here, was this. She bent down, and her breasts, round, firm, yeast-smelling, skimmed his face, then pressed into his neck, then chest.

Bard tasted sweet saliva on the center of Melissa's tongue, the mineral flavor of hard groundwater. He licked the salt from her greasy eyelids. She shook.

The chopper, still there, swept past, drawing broad strokes of vibrating sound over the roof of the Orphanage, over their heads.

And Melissa, her mind a cacophony of phrases, of clichés and justifications, crawled under Bardy, so she could press up toward the sound in the sky, a rhythm, a tickling, glowing vibration on which she could focus. "This is love," the phrases, sifting themselves, settled down to tell her. Bard (it gladdened her) couldn't keep himself from looking. He touched, he tasted, he pinched, and he pulled back, propping his elbow in the dirt and his head in that hand, to stare. She saw her body in his eyes, and knew it was beautiful. And inside. Her inside as his fingers found it again, welled round. "We're beautiful on the inside, Bard," she said, emphatically. And what the hell was she talking about? She and Bard? Two dirty, b.o.-smelling kids from Chicago? She kissed the wound on his eye. YEAH! And something more. She was talking about, feeling, something even more to it. How she was a part of womanhood, and it wasn't a bit funny. And then, God (was God here?), Bard found her clitoris. And it told her, and the sky told her, and the humming chopper, and the smell of the pine sap, and the smell of Bard—something sharp, something fresh like chlorophyll in cut grass—and all women, mothers and ancestors, "Bardy," she pulled his hard penis toward her, "put it inside."

And Bard rolled in, and so, there were no insides and outsides of kids. Because the chopper swelled, soft, hard, sweepingly inside her, thanks to Bard. "Ugh," she said truly surprised. And this was crazy, and this was NOT just her body. And her body was a deep, shining blue, star-pocked universe, and all women's bodies—hers—were round like sky, and she felt herself rise above the ground, beyond Bard's thrusting. And her smart hand dug down and found her own clitoris, and her smart teeth bit Bard's neck. And there was one distinct line, swirling, a milky way, linking all live things, sweeping birds, and swirling fishes, and the eyes of all embryos blinked, and Bardy—little, jerking Bardy, had never, really, even ever been born.

"I love you, Bard," but it was like talking to a jumping puppy.

"I'm coming!" he cried, and she laughed at him.

"No shit."

And, for Bard, for both Bards (big and little), THIS WAS HIS RHYTHM AND HIS BIGNESS, and a lifetime of all the Bards he had shed, who he'd thought had died: a bawling, baby Bard; a schoolyard demon; a gang-banger Bard; Shankus (a stabbing Bard); the hating Bard; Jail Bard; and even (some joke, until, maybe now) rehabilitated Bard—for all of them, the pain (he swellingly felt and remembered it) burst free, an embarrassing, shuddering, remembered, denied upheaval, and ("Mom"—he almost said that fucking word) and dear God, surely God loved him, surely God had been saving this up for one bad, stinking boy, because it consumed him in the moment. Then he, new, shed it all. He rolled off her.

His muscles, his hands and feet, his every bone, and skin, his temples, his brain, his head, felt the sweet, gentle, keen, true simplicity of living. The air on his skin was excruciating. His pain-freed body was soft, in pure softness, vulnerable to the roaming, lingering tingles. When Melissa came in close to kiss his chest, he waved her off him; no, this he could not stand.

"Let's eat," he told Melissa. "Put your clothes on. You're shivering; you're shaking, baby."

"Don't call me that." Because Melissa was a woman, wise, through and through.

"We can go the Blue Plate Cafe."

"And eat eggs?"

"Yeah. Scrambled."

"I'm dead. Carry me, Bard." She was joking, but he scooped her up, then dropped her.

"Wait," and she climbed on his back.

And Bardy, BIGNESS, steel of arm and leg, did carry her four blocks, a new man (they played and laughed and played), the whole way.

THE REVEREND W. C. THADDEUS

James A. Wiggins

For reasons he felt were unnecessary to fully contemplate and understand, Rev. W. C. Thaddeus, self-ordained Baptist minister, was always preoccupied by keen memories of sexual intercourse with his sister Henriette. And even though they dogged him day and night, they were, nevertheless, pleasant memories, memories swept up in sudden surges of lust that he found increasingly difficult to suppress, a lust so demanding of satisfaction that it required the cooperative efforts of both hands, each working tirelessly on his sustained erections, thus allowing the torrential rapids of his semen to flood the dry, barren, white plains of toilet paper.

They were also welcomed memories, spicing his imagination, heightening his curiosity on those blessed occasions whenever his eyes seized a seven- or eight- or nine-year-old girl in the act of picking at a scab on her knee or reaching down and pulling her socks up over her ankles. Over the years and to this very day, they were memories that busied his mind during long waits in dental offices, train stations, bus depots, barber shops, grocery check-out counters, luncheonettes, and especially in that closet-of-a-bedroom he rented from Mrs. Blanche Crockett for five dollars and fifty cents a week—memories that often took control of the steering wheel and parked his car outside the chain-linked fence of a schoolyard and waited patiently to offer some little girl a ride home. For that reason, the glove compartment was always well stocked with a supply of cherry-flavored lollipops.

And even as he listened abstractly to the wailing confessions of neighborhood sinners who came regularly each Sunday afternoon to Bible study in Mrs. Crockett's front-room parlor, Rev. W. C. Thaddeus's mind would always recreate the rolling wheatfields of his papa's farm near Shawnee County, Oklahoma. He was seventeen then, the oldest son among ten children. Henriette was the baby of the family, only nine years old and, of course, just as eager as her big brother, if not more so, to indulge in the unbridled pleasures that were of her flesh. And she was mentally retarded and bowlegged and cross-eyed and buck-toothed and slovenly, and didn't have any breasts yet to speak of.

It was always somewhere beneath the orange globe of a summer sun and in a secluded spot in the golden fields of wheat far and away from the opened shutters of the farmhouse windows and the smokehouse and the tractor shed that Rev. W. C. Thaddeus would help Henriette out of her clothes and plow with gigantic thrusts into his little sister's tight, wet vagina.

For reasons too befuddled by their own reasons for taking up space in his mind, Rev. W. C. Thaddeus could not imagine what it would be like to have sex with a woman; the idea was as alien to him as the thought of having sex with a broken chicken egg. Developed breasts, fleshy hips, pubic hairs, knowledgeable lips, inquisitive hands, embracing arms and thighs laced with perfume—the very thought of these body parts interacting with his own frightened him to no end, both individually and collectively in their physical manifestation of an adult female body. Unthinkable also was sex with a man or a boy. Why? He simply didn't know why and, for that matter, didn't care to know why either. It just seemed so perfectly natural and satisfying to him that his sexual development actually progressed along the path that it did, beginning first at the age of eleven with the cunts of pigs, then goats, then cows, and finally coming to full maturity on that sunny day when his papa aimed a double-barreled shotgun at three hired field hands lined up against the farm wall and ordered little Henriette to point out the no-count son-of-a-bitch who got her in the family way.

Now, exactly what happened on that sunny day in Rev. W. C. Thaddeus's biography has remained somewhat foggy in his memory to this third of August 1957. However, a fragment of an image from that day's events would sometimes intrude upon his awareness for no apparent reason: a locomotive train tugging boxcars and a red caboose, puffing white smoke, and racing on the horizon where blue sky and a field of golden wheat merged to form a pencil-sharp black line. And the train whistle would go *whooo-whooo-whooooo!* in shrilled, quick outbursts inside his head. And a few other things like the BOOM! BOOM! BOOM! of a shotgun somewhere in the far-off distances of his brain, and the zinging sound of buckshots as if whizzing past his ears would, though rarely, pierce the quietude of his dreamless sleeps. And from such sleeps he would often awake, tangled in damp sheets, startled for no apparent reason that he could think of; shaking like a leaf, he would breathe hard as if he had been running for his life. In such an alarmed and confused state of mind, it seemed to him as though his upright body actually swayed in bed to the rocking motion of a boxcar. And his head would resound with the clickety-clack, clickety-clack, clickety-clack of a locomotive train clickety-clacking at top speed. *Whooo-whooo-whooooo!*

But what Rev. W. C. Thaddeus did remember clearly and yearn for most during the past twenty years since leaving Oklahoma was the pure and unaffected spirituality of his brief affair with Henriette. Those tantalizing memories of pulling himself out of his sister's hairless cunt would always convince him more than ever before that he was a man destined for glory. Blissful glory pure and simple. And if he wasn't sure of anything else about his life and the world order around him, he was steadfast in this, his conviction: *I'm a man for whom God, in His divine power and wisdom, has created a special glory, a glory that's tailor-made for me and nobody else.*

When Rev. W. C. Thaddeus did dream, he always dreamt of his glory. It would show itself as a radiant ball of white light in a void of utter blackness. It was a dazzling, heavenly glory that he would often fantasize as hovering slightly above his head, showering his entire body in an avalanche of little gold-silver sparks as he prowled the lonely streets of the neighborhood at night. Whenever sitting alone in public places, he would imagine himself cocooned in a blaze of shimmering glory and attracting the eyes of total strangers. He fancied them gravitating toward him, admiring his glory, engaging in brisk delightful chit-chat with him, opening their homes to him, thus allowing him to meet interesting people and potential life-long friends.

Now, to what practical use he would put this glory in the service of humanity once he got hold of it was not so pressing a problem as finding it in the first place. And why God, in His divine power and wisdom, hid Rev. W. C. Thaddeus's glory inside some little girl's pussy was a question the Reverend had long ago chalked off to his religious faith. It definitely qualified, in his opinion, as one of these great religious mysteries of all time—like the Virgin Birth, just to name a good example. But the all-consuming, nagging question that had hounded him over the years since leaving Oklahoma was, *Which little pussy?* This strange and wonderful world was full of virgin pussies. White ones, black ones, brown ones, yellow ones, red ones . . . not to mention albino ones. Millions of virginal pairs of genital lips, each one with its own pink tongue-of-a-clitoris shyly poking out, each one dewy with the sour smell and taste of little girl's urine. Why, just thinking about these virgin pussies was more than enough to drive any sane man crazy.

Over the years Rev. W. C. Thaddeus did just that and ONLY that—think about his glory tucked inside one in a million, possibly one in a billion, virgin pussies. Numerous were the nights when he would toss and turn in his bed wherever that was in these United States of America and cry out in agony: *Oh Lord and Savior, my Redeemer. Where is the little pussy Thou hath buried thy gift of glory in? I pray Thou wilt guide me in finding it quickly and in peace. As I go about my daily search, please help and comfort me. Give me the courage, give me the strength to endure the inevitable trials and errors. Protect me always from hopelessness and despair. Keep me safe from harm's way, especially from the police and the jailhouse door. Oh God, where is that little pussy? In Jesus' name, I pray for an answer. Amen.*

Protected from hopelessness and despair by daily prayer, Rev. W. C. Thaddeus went about his search for glory across America's midwestern region, selling miniature Bibles at two dollars each, three for five, seven for ten. Wandering from one camp revival meeting to another, preaching the Gospel, spreading the good news of how God so loved the world that He sent his only begotten son to suffer in this world and die on the cross for our sins and misdemeanors.

Through endless trials and errors and with all the missionary zeal of a man in search of the Holy Grail, he plundered scores of laced bloomers. Stalking and sniffing about the river roads and small country towns and big cities, he ripped his way into underpants and plundered without mercy or tenderness, leaving behind a trail of bleeding and traumatized little girls, some as young as four years; and still his goal, his reward—in other words, his glory—remained as elusive as before, hanging out of his grasping fingers' reach like a carrot dangling from the tip of a wooden pole. But he wasn't discouraged—not by no means. He was, after all, you see, a man of faith who smiled in the face of disappointment as he snatched himself out of some dry, gloryless vagina; indeed, he was a man who always got back on his feet again and zipped up his pants in a hurry and continued his journey of spiritual fulfillment, smiling in the faces of girls he met along the way whose double-dutch jump-roping was right on cue.

Colorado, Nebraska, Wyoming, Arkansas—he searched for his glory in these and other lands, nourished by the deep conviction that his Lord and Savior did not grant glory to those who were plagued by doubts, frustrations, alarms, fears. He attributed his success in outrunning the long legs of the law to none other than—who else?—God. And for that he was extremely grateful and prayed on his knees just before laying himself down to sleep: *I thank Thee, oh Lord and Savior, my Redeemer. Keep me always safe from those who would persecute me for no good reason at all. In Jesus' name, I pray for everlasting protection. Amen.*

But wait a minute!

Hold your horses!

Just hold the phone, please!

Why this sudden rush to judgment?

To turn your head away in disgust and call it nothing more than the wholesale rape of little girls was to miss the point entirely. Rather, you see, Rev. W. C. Thaddeus likened it to a nationwide inspection of the effectiveness of the country's electrical utilities and himself to a 100-watt light bulb engineered by his Redeemer for the sole purpose of screwing America's younger sockets, thus bringing light (if an electrical current were indeed present) to an otherwise dark and desolate corner on the planet Earth.

These sockets were mostly the young daughters of divorced or unmarried big-breasted women who saw in him a man who gave them crisp, multifolded ten dollar bills without asking for anything in return. Lonely women they were who had a soft spot for the retiring, shy type; so Rev. W. C. Thaddeus fitted into the scheme of their daily lives right from the start. You see, he knew how to pick them.

But first and foremost, they were women who knew him as just plain Thaddeus, a man whom they saw took pleasure in the simple things in life, a man who was given to philosophical reflections on the absurdity of human happiness in a world of sin, a man who wanted nothing more than to be left alone to watch TV all day—a man who didn't mind at all sleeping on the sofa and keeping a watchful eye on their daughters while they (these big-breasted women of various ages and skin complexions) bar-hopped the city's taverns and cocktail lounges. And when they returned home arm-in-arm with total strangers . . . well, they became (as it turned out) women who introduced Thaddeus as their long-lost brother newly found and newly arrived from Colorado. No, that wasn't it. Tennessee? South Dakota? Arizona? Nebraska? Well then, why not Missouri? Oh, shoot! They tried and tried and tried again; they could never get it right to save their necks.

Okay . . . how about Jamaica? Cuba? Panama?

Anyway, women they most certainly were who moaned, grunted, and gasped as they got fucked by total strangers and as the bedroom door stood wide open while their little daughters looked on scared half out of their wits.

Loud moaning and fast breathing. The rhythmic squeaking of the bedsprings. The air heavy with the smell of body odor. Head, arms, and legs flopping about the bed and completely out of control beneath the lurching broad back and shoulders of a naked stranger—beneath the sweating, muscular, pumping buttocks and wrenching thighs of a naked man who huffed and puffed and yelled at the top his lungs: GIVE IT UP, BITCH! GIVE IT UP, BITCH! GIVE IT UP, BITCH! Every one of these women, these mothers of little girls, would clench the bedsheets and squeal out in a voice husky with passion, "Oooooh Gawd! Oooooh Gawd! Oooooh Gawd! For Christ's sake, Thaddeus, get your . . . get your . . . get your ass in here now! Oooooh, now Thaddeus! Oooooh Gawd! Oooooh, now Thaddeus! Oooooh Gawd!"

Stopping whatever it was he was doing, usually mopping the kitchen floor, Thaddeus would storm into the bedroom where the woman got fucked in full view of her wide-eyed, teary little daughters. He would kneel beside the bed where the woman's head hung loose and bobbed wildly over the edge as she got fucked by a naked man whose lurching broad back raised increasingly higher and higher as his arms became straighter and straighter, whose meaty fingers clawed deeper and deeper into those huge breasts of hers. For a minute or three, Thaddeus would struggle as best he could under the circumstances to synchronize the jerky bobbing of his own head with that of the woman's so that he could put his lips against her ear and keep them there while she got fucked as if there was no tomorrow. Then, and *only* then, could he give her what she had screamed her heart out for while he was busy mopping the kitchen floor a few minutes ago; *only* then could he whisper into her ear what she was in need of beneath the huffing, puffing, fucking, quivering stranger; *only* in violent moments of great, climactic, pelvic heavings and hitchings on the bed would the woman even think of, indeed, insist on hearing one of Thaddeus's *Oooooh!* so soothing, ear-whispered discourses on the virtues of Platonic love. Years later, Rev. W. C. Thaddeus came to view these big-breasted women with his utmost contempt.

He was reminiscing once again on the possible whereabouts of his glory one fine summer day in Chicago, Illinois—well, as a matter of fact, it was yesterday around three o'clock when he was reminiscing on the South Side of the city where he happened to linger butt-naked by his window overlooking Lafayette Avenue. He stooped and held back the curtains and glanced up and across the street. He wasn't looking for anything in particular when lo and behold, miracle of miracles, his eyes were blessed this day by the sight of a little girl somersaulting on the sidewalk in front of a yellow frame house. A spasm of sexual joy gripped his balls and stretched out his penis. Even from this distance of three or four doors, he was sure this girl wore no underpants. The brown-sugar skin of her inner thighs ran smooth and uninterrupted all the way to that tiny, hairless slit-of-a-cunt in her crotch. He was certain of this.

The little girl somersaulted again.

Great God A'mighty! Will you get a load of that!

And for a flicker of a second, she was heels-over-head without any bloomers on, her legs spread wide in thin air like the spokes of a wheel. She now stood right-side-up again, her blue cotton dress having fallen into place but not before Rev. W. C. Thaddeus had imprinted deep inside his brain an image of her socket, a socket he believed was electrified by the power of his glory; indeed, he was convinced he had at long last found the only virgin pussy that would enable him to fuck his way into immortality. Pressing his nose against the window screen, he clutched his bare chest and choked on his heart.

A small-breasted woman wearing a green scarf around her head stepped out onto the yellow-painted porch and gestured with a quick flick of her hand for the little girl to come right this second inside the house . . . NOW!

"She must be the mother," Reverend W. C. Thaddeus heard his voice saying.

He let go of the curtains and straightened up weak and trembling. He was so happy to be butt-naked at such an opportune time as this with his sweating back leaning against the wall by the window. He was so happy that he could only think of just how happy, happy, happy he was; and from the pit of his belly he released a gurgling cry and did something he had never done before in his life: he ejaculated without the assistance of his hands. A distinct *squoink*! sound was emitted from the mouth of his penis at the precise moment that a stringy blob of semen shot halfway across this closet of a room. Near the foot of the bed and in the center of Mrs. Crockett's silk oriental rug, the pearl-colored blob, and in the noonday sunlight that filtered through the curtains, the blob also glistened.

In no time flat he was hard again. No, not his penis but his brain—he was thinking hard, whirling up scraps of information he had thrown away as trash a long time ago in the alleys of his mind. True, the little girl was known to him and had been seen by him numerous times playing hopscotch outside that yellow frame house on this street where he had resided as Mrs. Crockett's roomer for the past two years. She was seven or eight or so, he thought, he hoped; but unlike those other occasions when her hair was a mess of black ashen wool over her head, the bloom-erless girl he had just witnessed a moment ago appeared reasonably well groomed: one fat pigtail on top of her head, one shorter pigtail sticking out on each side.

Oh, how in heaven's name could I have been so blind? And to think my glory was right here all this time in my own back yard and under my nose!

Rev. W. C. Thaddeus chided himself for forgetting what no right-thinking man would have forgotten as mere scraps, like the scattered pages of a newspaper tossed by a gust of wind, swept up and across the window of his consciousness where they clung, reminding him of last summer's tent revival meeting on the vacant lot, of his sermon on the evils of policy racketeering, and of his prohibition to the neighbors to never, never, never step foot inside the yellow frame house on pains of eternal damnation—*why, of course, my little darling is the daughter of a policy racketeer*!

Then it occurred to his spinning mind that he must have lost forever the piece of crumpled paper he had written the girl's name on.

Oh well, I'll just ask Mrs. Crockett at the very first opportunity.

PLOT TEST

Serafina Chamberlin

At 7:45 Monday morning, Emma stamped into the front entryway of Wallner Prep, tracking snow behind her. She tried to ignore the fatigue floating in her stomach along with half a pot of strong coffee. After staying up most of the night the previous Thursday taking her mother to the emergency room to cast the arm Connie broke in a drunken fall, Emma had skipped classes on Friday, pretending to herself she'd catch up on days of undone homework. Instead, Emma had spent much of the weekend either out of the house or brooding over why Connie would not speak to her.

Emma stood pulling off her gloves and inhaling warm air as the dean made his ceremonial walk to post the results of Friday's basketball game. With an eight-foot posterboard clamped in his left armpit, Karl T. Hofacker strolled the first-floor hall, using his unneeded walking stick to splash greetings towards various students as they parted before him, clearing to the sides of the hall.

"Hey, Brasler, hair's getting a little long there, don't you think?"

"Come on, Mr. Hofacker, dress code was dropped three years ago," the pimply-faced senior shot back bravely.

Hofacker paused and darted the top of his stick against the boy's chest. "Fought that harder than anything I could name. Even harder than I argued to fly the flag at half-mast for Kent State."

Emma tore her eyes away from the lunch menu posted on the "Class of '77" easel bulletin board and snuck a look down the hall. She didn't want any encounters with Hofacker today. His good 'ole boy demeanor hadn't fooled Emma since her first month at Wallner. Hofacker had accosted her in the lunchroom, barking, "I hear you're a Saxon, young lady. Are you the last of your line?"

Emma felt her chin shoot up defiantly, in the tradition of a long list of young ons. "Yeah, I am."

"Thank God!" the dean had said and stomped off in his high-top yellow hiking , leaning on his walking stick.

ofacker was almost to the front of the main staircase when Roger Peterman, r who was never without his yellow highliter and Indian beaded belt, stepped into the dean's path. "Ah, Mr. Hofacker, I need to talk to you."

"Well, make an appointment, son." Hofacker didn't like rituals interrupted.

"No, that's not necessary, I just need to explain about the four classes I missed last week." Roger was walking backward now, trying to keep up with Hofacker's brisk progress.

"Peterman, get *out* of my way!" Hofacker bellowed, and the boy's shoulders slumped as he stumbled to the side of the hall and leaned against a locker, his eyes fixed on his black high tops. Hofacker would not remember this encounter the following spring when Roger Peterman hanged himself just before graduation.

Emma felt safe as Karl Hofacker reached the end of the hall and turned to go up the stairs. But then he whirled his head around to look back at her. "Emma Saxon, you tell those brothers of yours I'm still looking for the ringers for the hall bells. I hear rumors, and the statute of limitations hasn't run out yet."

Emma blushed, not sure if he was teasing her. She couldn't think of a response, but it didn't matter, as the old man mounted the first flight of steps two stairs at a time. At the landing he raised his stick over his head and used it as a lever to knock last week's basketball placard down. Emma smiled and her hot face cooled as Hofacker leaned his walking stick against the wall with irritation in order to struggle with the flopping posterboard he wanted to post. Just as he hooked one of the pre-punched holes onto one of the nails eight feet up the wall, Maria's voice blew in with a gust of cold air behind Emma.

"Jesus, another maudlin assessment of why we're not gonna make it to state again this year," Maria said, and planted her hiking boots one behind the other on the soaked carpet runner, leaning back slightly as she watched Hofacker. Her stance and wrinkled-nose expression exuded what-the-hell-is-the-old-lunatic-up-to-now, and Emma laughed.

Just as the dean barely scraped the posterboard against the second hook, the other end came loose and flopped to the floor. "Goddamn it to hell!" Hofacker spat, and the two girls covered their mouths and whirled around, feigning extreme interest in the bulletin board. After a moment, Maria said out of the corner of her mouth, "What makes Hofacker think we're interested in stupid comments like, 'It was over so quickly it almost didn't hurt . . . but it did'?" Emma shifted her head slightly, looking at Maria out of the corner of her eye, and they arched their eyebrows at each other, meaning, in their long-established silent language, *We are correct to think we're smarter than all this bullshit, aren't we?* As Maria blew on her fingers, they relaxed their stances, Emma with one hand resting on top of the bulletin board.

"Goddamn cold out today," Maria said, and unwound a long black scarf from her hair. She waved a manicured hand towards the bulletin board. "Anything urgent I need to know, and how was your trip to Randy's and, and, that woman's house?"

Emma laughed. "First, there's cheese pizza today in the snack bar, Christmas break won't be any longer than previously announced, no deaths. Second, my visit with Randy and *Amy* was good. Your jealousy is showing, by the way."

"Fine." Maria tossed her hair back with mock drama. "I just always assumed Randy would wait for me."

Emma adjusted her backpack on her shoulder. "Well, he's always been fond of you, but, I don't know. Eight years, Maria. Besides, I can't swear to it, but I think my mother may have warned him off. What are you doing here so early, anyway? You don't have an eight o'clock."

"How *are* things with your mom?" Maria had heard the whole story over cinnamon coffee on Friday night.

Emma shrugged in response, studying the tips of her boots. "Still the same. I got home last night and just went upstairs. She never said a word."

Maria rushed on to another subject. "I'm here 'cause I gotta go to the bib—I have to finish that paper for Andrews. Did you finish *Return of the Native*?" (In eighth grade Emma and Maria had started using the French word for library— "bibliotheque," and after a short stay at "biblio," had finally abbreviated it to "bib".)

"Well, not exactly," Emma grimaced. "God, Hardy is so damn boring."

Maria scanned the bulletin board and shook her head. "No, he's not. *Tess of the D'Urbervilles* is really good." She looked Emma in the eye. "Gonna be able to pass the plot test?"

Emma shrugged again. "You just like Hardy 'cause Andrews told you how you remind him of Tess. Jesus, Maria, you could just lie down on his desk and get an A."

Maria gave her a cold look. "Not funny, Em."

Emma sighed. "Sorry. I'm just gonna flunk this test, and I'm so goddamn tired. I didn't get much sleep this weekend."

Maria poked her with an elbow. "I know. Want to go to the Medici for pizza at lunch?"

"No, I'm going to try and finish the book during lunch." The weight of this lie lodged in Emma's upper chest. Having read only fifty pages, she wasn't likely to finish the book in a week, much less a lunch period.

They turned towards the library just as Hofacker finished admiring his handiwork and started down the stairs. On the second step he stopped and scowled at the neat stacks of books and notebooks edging each wide stair. "Haven't I told you little shits," Hofacker bellowed, as students' heads snapped in his direction, "not to leave your crap on the stairs!" With that he kicked the nearest pile, and descended the stairs, crisscrossing back and forth, kicking or shoving with his walking stick each book he found in his path. A couple of students foolishly reached through the metal banisters to attempt a rescue of their possessions before they joined the cascade, while others ran to gather the hundreds of airborne notebook sheets, and Emma and Maria froze momentarily, both terrified of laughing.

A freshman boy rounded the stair landing, got a full view of the mayhem in the lobby and retreated back upstairs again, which proved too much for Emma. Holding her breath, her face working to keep straight, Emma grabbed Maria's arm, pulling her towards the library entrance. Before the door shut behind them, Emma and Maria heard Hofacker yell, "Now get all this shit cleaned up, PRONTO!"

Under the sharp irritated looks of the librarians, Emma and Maria laughed breathlessly, until Emma finally said, "I have to get to algebra—I'll see you later." She ducked out the rear entrance of the library, a wide grin still on her face.

Dorrie Bleeker hadn't finished her tuna sandwich at lunch again, and smelling it, Emma wondered how many molding crusts were in that backpack, anyway. Her empty stomach rolled, both from the odor and fatigue. It had been pointless to try and read further in *Return of the Native* instead of eating lunch.

With tremendous effort, Emma focused her eyes onto the test in front of her. Dorrie scratched her pencil along with busy purpose, but Emma just thought wearily over and over, *I'm screwed, I'm just plain screwed.* How could she pass a plot test when she'd only read seventy-five pages? Emma laid her cheek down on the desk and curled her arm around her head. Some of the questions were the usual taunts, *In what country is* Return of the Native *set? Bangladesh,* Emma thought sarcastically, but scrawled in the answer. It was still snowing, and Emma could hear the shouts of the public school kids playing. *Why didn't we get a snow day today?* she thought with a vehemence that surprised her. The wall clock across the room over Mr. Geraldson's head ticked with an unnatural loudness and Emma wished for a moment that it would fall and hit the teacher—with any luck, cancelling the test. This thought was enough to make her smile in a way that told Geraldson she wasn't thinking about Thomas Hardy, and he scowled, turning a pencil end over end in his hands.

Emma skipped the next two questions as hopeless and straightened up, stretching. She tried to concentrate on what little she knew about Thomas Hardy's heath, but instead saw in the blank white spaces of her test Connie sitting on the couch under the light. Last night when Emma returned from the north side, she'd barely noticed her mother's matted hair and dirty nightgown, but the martini on the end table zoomed, threatening to engulf the living room, the cocktail onions turning into meteors. *She isn't supposed to be drinking,* Emma thought. When Connie did not respond to her "Hi, I'm back," Emma kept her mouth shut about mixing the painkillers.

Then Emma had turned on her heel and mounted the two flights of stairs in silence as every other Saxon had at one time or another, leaving the hell of the first floor behind. Halfway up the first flight, Emma's mood changed from worried to angry, and she thought, *What the hell did I do anyway? Why does she continually pull this crap with me for no reason? I take care of her when she's fucking drunk, listen to the doctor's lecture, and she acts as if the whole thing's my fault!* By halfway up the second flight, her shoulders slumped with despair, and she sat on the top step unlacing her boots with numb fingers, wishing for rescue. When she was five, Emma had thought for a long time that Paul McCartney would show up to be her one True Friend, but he seemed to have lost the directions to Hyde Park. As the hopelessness surrounded her, Emma got up to turn on the radio—loud—and left her backpack unopened on the landing.

"Emma. Emma Saxon." Her head snapped up. Geraldson's bald forehead wrinkled into folds and flushed bright red. He tapped his eyeglasses on his knee deliberately and Emma returned his stare for a moment. "In my office after class, Emma." She nodded and ducked her head again, catching Dorrie Bleeker's narrowed-eye sidelong glance. Emma slid her right hand across her lap and rested it on her thigh, middle finger outstretched for Dorrie's benefit, who sniffed and slipped her eyes back to her paper.

Emma studied her test once more. *Which of his five senses does Clym Yeobright eventually damage by overwork?* Emma considered her twenty percent chance of guessing correctly, remembered the character was a teacher, and wrote *eyesight*. She looked at the clock, anxiety rising in her throat. The period was nearly over, and besides flunking the test, Emma would be done for the day and she'd have to go home and face Connie's silence. Emma doodled irradiation around the word "fate" in the question *Who are Eustacia and Wildeve and what is their fate?* and wondered about Geraldson. He's barely spoken to Emma since praising her paper on *Franny and Zooey* in late September. Emma wrote *Eustacia is Clym's wife and Wildeve runs the inn* and yawned. She had no idea what became of them. *Clym shoots Eustacia and Wildeve and puts us all out of our misery,* Emma thought and stretched again, drawing a glower from Mr. Geraldson. *What is that asshole's problem? And why is Mom being such a bitch this time?* Emma thought, looking at the empty space on her paper. She remembered the standardized tests in her public grammar school, and the tough kids who bragged they'd filled in the answer sheet blanks in the shape of some design, like a Christmas tree. One of those kids had recently won a color television in an essay contest and the Hyde Park *Herald* had run her picture. Funny, Emma thought. *Theresa Collins, who had tits and dressed like a hooker from sixth grade on because all she ever wanted since the first day of kindergarten when she slammed in late was for someone to notice her, discovers she can write, and I, supposedly so smart and so much more privileged, am flunking yet another test.* Emma smiled and sketched a small evergreen in the corner of her paper.

"Sit down, Emma," Mr. Geraldson said, indicating his desk chair. He sat on the desk, towering above Emma. His face furrowed into what she recognized as his "serious" look. *His face would probably crack like paper maché if he ever truly smiled,* Emma thought.

Geraldson picked up a book off the desk, and leafing through the pages, not looking at Emma, said, "You cheated on the test, didn't you?"

Emma flushed hotly. This was the last accusation she was expecting. Since the quarter was almost over, she'd wondered whether she might get a lecture on attitude, or be treated to one of Geraldson's rambling speeches about how values were so much better in his home state of Montana. When Emma answered, her voice was cold, but uncertain and sounded far away. "No. No, Mr. Geraldson, I didn't."

Geraldson slammed the book down on the desk. "Don't you dare lie to me, Emma."

Emma jumped and leaned back away from Geraldson. She picked up a piece of Ko-Rec-Type from the edge of the desk. As she worried it between her thumb and her forefinger, white flecks clung and spread over her hands like a rare and peculiar cancer.

The door opened and one of the other English teachers came into the shared office. Hal London had been Emma's freshman teacher and she smiled up into his gray eyes, looking for rescue. London started to smile back, but with an almost imperceptible shake of his head, Geraldson threw Emma's life preserver back to shore. Hal London merely said, "Emma," as he passed behind her chair, and her eyes dimmed with tears.

"We're here, Emma, to give you a chance to explain, so if I were you, I'd make the most of it." Geraldson regarded Emma over the tops of his glasses and caught his walrus moustache in his lower teeth, waiting.

"I didn't cheat. There's nothing to explain."

"Come off it! I don't buy it, Emma! I know you didn't even *open Return of the Native*." Geraldson leaned his face down to Emma's level. Without thinking, Emma shoved her chair back away from his bloodshot eyes.

She took a deep breath. "O.K., Mr. Geraldson, so maybe I didn't quite finish the book, but—"

"Didn't finish the damn book! Aha, the truth will out, eh, young lady?" Spittle beaded Geraldson's moustache.

Unable to mask the defiance in her voice, Emma demanded, "What makes you think I cheated, anyway?"

"I saw you, Emma. I saw you stretch, over and over, so you could look at Dorrie's test."

Emma stared at him, disbelief widening her eyes, and barked a laugh. "I was stretching because I'm *tired*, Mr. Geraldson. I never once looked at Dorrie's paper. I was looking over at her because her backpack reeked of tunafish, and—"

"Yeah, sure, Emma. Why don't you just admit that you don't care about this class or about school? You waltz in with an arrogant attitude, comment when you feel like it or have bothered to read the book, but never really join in. You hold yourself back and regard us all as peons who aren't as smart as you. I had high hopes for you in September, but you just dropped the ball, and have refused to go the extra ten yards all quarter."

Emma's spine felt brittle, and the heat of a shocked flush crept over her belly. She couldn't believe Geraldson really thought all these things about her. *I do care, I do care,* she wanted to scream. *Of course I care—books are my salvation, my only hope,* Emma thought as desperation—what she could only describe as complete emptiness—flooded her stomach and sweat broke out along her hairline. She gripped the edges of the chair under her thighs, and wished she was outside, in the snow, where she could cool off.

"If you don't admit to me that you cheated, Emma, I'm going to flunk you this quarter, and you'll have to make it up by doubling up your senior year." Emma stared up at him, her panic deepening, and he nodded, then smiled—she couldn't believe it, he actually smiled. "Make your choice wisely, Emma. Give it some consideration —I'll give your parents a call tonight. I think they'll be pretty interested in your exploits. Really, I would think you'd be ashamed to be so lackadaisical, with a pro-fessor for a father and a professional mother."

Rage rose in Emma's throat. Her ragged voice leapt out, stunning her as she stood up, now eye-level with Geraldson. "You go right ahead and call 'em, *Mister* Geraldson. You'll have to make a couple of calls, though—my father doesn't live with us anymore—my mother kicked him out when I was eleven. If you're lucky,

Mom might even be sober when you reach her, but I doubt it. My 'professional mother' has been home all day with a broken arm because she fell on her face last Thursday after a dance with a couple of martinis." Emma stopped for breath, unaware of the tears on her face. Hal London had turned around at his desk and watched her, his face creased with concern, but Geraldson's head was bent. "So, *get your facts straight,* Mr. Geraldson, or *run it up the flagpole and see who salutes, wouldja?*" Her voice was her armor, her weapon, an icepick, stabbing again and again.

Emma shrugged into her down jacket and picked up her backpack, swiping away tears. "No, I didn't finish the book. But I also didn't cheat, Mr. Geraldson. Because if I'm as smart as you seem to think I am, didn't it occur to you that I would do a better job of copying off Dorrie—she probably had all the right answers and half of my test is blank, isn't it?" Her voice rose another notch. "I didn't finish the book because I was too busy talking to emergency room doctors about my drunken mother—too busy with *real life,* goddamn it!"

Emma turned around at the door, and this time Geraldson met her eyes, his own filled with clouded emotions. The sureness of her voice faltered then. "If you'll just be decent, Mr. Geraldson, and come up with another plot test, I'll be ready to take it Friday." She paused, and wished she hadn't put on her jacket. Sweat rolled down her back. "But I guess if you want to tell Mr. Stephens and Mr. Hofacker that I cheated, go right ahead. I'm not afraid of anything at Wallner. The only thing I'm afraid of, Mr. Geraldson, is opening the front door at home. See you, Mr. London," Emma threw her backpack over her shoulder and dove out the door.

Emma stumbled off campus, slipping through the snow, and hurried along 58th Street, her jacket hanging open, her breath gasping out in front of her. Sure now that Geraldson would have her expelled from Wallner, she just wanted to get her bedroom door locked before her mother found out. Emma turned south on Dorchester and practically ran the last half-block. It wasn't until she fought through the untrimmed hedges adrift in snow at the end of the walk that a reassuring thought bloomed in Emma's mind. *Maybe they'll believe me.* Emma stopped on the bottom step to the porch, slowly becoming aware of the cold. *Maybe if they believe me, things will change.* Her breath calmed. Hugging her jacket closed, Emma mounted the last four stairs in two large steps and slammed into the house.

Without stopping to check if Connie was talking to her yet, Emma retreated to her room, shed her outer clothes and dropped Carole King's "Tapestry" album onto the turntable before flopping onto the bed. She rested her chin on the edge of the mattress and studied the lemon-yellow poster next to the window, which read "Not To Decide Is To Decide" in red lettering meant to look like graffiti. When the colors ran together in front of her transfixed eyes, she blinked several times and rolled onto her back.

Emma threw an arm across her forehead and thought, *Shit, what have I done now*? The blossom of certainty she had felt on the porch withered a little. She detested losing her temper, especially because now Geraldson knew how truly horrible her insides were, making Mom right again. A flush of embarrassment spread over

Emma. *Jesus, if he thought I was a bitch before—*

She sat up, refusing to finish the thought. What she needed now was escape. The joint she'd bummed from Randy was packed tight and expertly rolled. Emma let the kitchen match burn longer than necessary, enjoying the flame licking closer and closer to her hand. Finally, she took in a chestful of smoke and lay back on the bed. One by one Emma shut down her emotions, crawling down to the emptiness she feared was her true center, floating into Carole King's voice.

FROG LESSONS

Jennifer G. Yos

The embryos came in the regular mail. Lana squished the water in the envelope back and forth, back and forth with her thumbs, that is, until she eyed the name FY-BRO in the return address.

"Oooh, the tadpoles!"

She winced. Maybe now she had damaged them with her careless squishing. The old woman read the label pasted to the outside of the envelope that warned "Open immediately upon arrival. Contains living organisms," and sprang into action, floorboards creaking faster than usual under her heavy shoes.

"*Apples*? What about *apples*?" Frank asked, his mouth agape as he looked up from his camera parts spread out upon the sunporch picnic table.

"No, Frank. TADPOLES!" Lana impatiently held the envelope up for her boarder to see, swaying side to side like an anchored tugboat with a mission. Frank shook his head at the sight of yet another mail order package. He didn't want to know what it was. He had stopped asking a long time ago. With Lana it could be anything. She'll get no encouragement from me, he told himself. He already knew two things for sure. One, whatever it was, she didn't need it, and two, it was sure to have a story to go along with it, one that he didn't care to hear. Lana could never cut right to the point. Everything had a story, a history. If a can of corn was on sale today, did Lana say, "Frank, corn was two for fifty-nine cents today"? No, not Lana. "Frank," she'd say, "you know that new grocery, the one that opened up next to the Thrifty Discount Bakery, the one that used to be Locke's Hardware before he sold it on account of his trouble with the IRS? Well, remember how we were wondering what the prices would be like, if they'd be any better than Bentley's Park and Shop, even though Bentley's does have lean meat and nice produce, but you have to pay for it? Well, I bought two cans of corn there, for that casserole dish Irma sent me last week through the Recipe Chain Letter . . . "

No, Frank decided to tune Lana out before she got started. He fiddled with his hearing aids, setting their volume all the way down, a trick he used when he didn't care to be disturbed, and began again to examine the jammed rewind mechanism on his camera. Lana saw him fiddling with the hearing aid and wondered if it was giving him trouble. She approached him from behind and spoke directly into his right ear.

"Frank, remember the frog hatchery kit? Look! The frog embryos are here! From the frog hatchery kit! They're here!" She set the envelope of frog embryos down on a cleared section of the picnic table before him.

"We're going to witness 'the miracle of frog metamorphosis'!" she continued, quoting the box from the frog hatchery kit. "Right here, on my sunporch!" Without taking his eyes off his camera, Frank waved away Lana's silently moving lips like he would shoo away an annoying mosquito at his ear.

She was always sending away for something she didn't need or entering contests where all you win is another contest. She spent half the morning licking stickers and placing them over circles. She had junk mail in piles, spilling, leaning, sliding everywhere—catalogues for homemade candy, wicker furniture, fancy dolls, frilly night clothes—you name it, Lana had a catalogue for it. And Lana joined every club she was invited to join like it was a social engagement. She joined one called the "Golden Years Book-of-the-Month Club." Turned out the golden years were between ages five and ten—they sent all nursery-rhyme and kiddie books. Lana read them anyway. One morning she read a story to him called "Timothy's Camera," about a young boy who received a camera for his seventh birthday. Seven-year-old Timothy took all kinds of pictures—one of an ant carrying a crumb across the sidewalk, one of his grandma without her teeth, one inside his closet at night to see if a ghost would show up on the negative—he had seen that happen in a scary movie, one of his dog laughing, one of his baby sister spitting out her strained vegetables. He shot twelve pictures in all, but when he opened up the back of the camera, he saw that he had forgotten to load the film. The roll was still wrapped in plastic in the styrofoam box. He cried and cried, and his mother tried to comfort him by saying "Now you can take twelve *new* pictures," but that didn't help. He wanted the pictures he had already taken. Finally, his grandma, who was wearing her teeth again, told him that he hadn't lost the pictures, really. They'd simply been captured on a different kind of film. Memory film, she called it. The memory film is in his head, she said, and she told him she had memory film in her head, too. It takes the most beautiful pictures, she told him. Pictures you can see, and hear, and smell, and taste, and feel over and over again . . . .

When she had finished reading the story to Frank, Lana looked up at him boldly and with one eyebrow raised asked, "What's on your memory film, Frank?"

"I don't know," Frank responded uncomfortably, uncrossing his arms, recrossing them, then uncrossing them again to pull a handkerchief out from his trouser pocket. He began polishing his glasses. His eyes looked small and weak without the glasses. They reminded Lana of the wandering and watery eyes of a newborn. "I think my memory film has an expiration date. I'm lucky if I remember what I had for breakfast this morning," he joked, ". . . but I damn well know I had coffee!"

The coffee reference was a mild tease aimed at Lana's membership in the Dutch Girl's Coffee-of-the-Month Club. Stacks of unopened coffee cans lined Lana's cellar walls. Lana's and Frank's one-cup-a-day limit trailed behind the Dutch Girl's monthly five-pound shipments long ago. It was also an attempt to change the subject. Frank refused to talk about anything from his past. "The past is the past," he'd say with finality. When he came to Lana looking for room and board eighteen years ago, he offered very little information about his situation. But Lana had already learned of Frank's forced retirement from Aldo's Lumber, of the unexpected death of his wife Eleanor, and of his estrangement from their only daughter, Natalie, whose promiscuous lifestyle Frank was convinced had caused his wife's heart failure. After three weeks of allowing him to sit at her sunporch picnic table doing absolutely nothing but staring at his hands clasped in front of him, one morning Lana strapped a Polaroid camera around his neck and pushed him off the sunporch into the back yard demanding a roll of photographs that would make her laugh. Minutes later, clattering the locked screen door, Frank claimed the camera was jammed. It took a while for him to convince her, but she finally let him back in and he spent the rest of the afternoon fixing her camera on the porch picnic table.

Lana finished explaining in detail the stages of tadpole life to her deaf boarder and then gave his shoulder a gentle squeeze. She bustled to the porch refrigerator where, standing tippy-toe, she reached for the frog hatchery tank stored in a box on top. Fingertips barely grasping its sides, she slid the box to the front of the icebox. That's when she felt the familiar pull. It felt like a giant air bubble travelling slowly and painfully through her heart. The box teetered above her head as she slowly drew in her breath. She turned to Frank, focusing on his plaid shirt hunched over the table top. Though she was paralyzed with pain, her only fear was that he might turn around now and see her. She didn't want him to know about her spells. They came on more often now, sometimes two or three times in one day, but she kept them secret. She knew he would insist on a doctor, and she wanted nothing to do with doctors or hospitals. She had finished with them a long time ago when she was just a girl, when Nature took away her baby too early. Nature she must accept. But doctors took away her chance of ever bearing any more children. No more doctors.

With hands still clutching the box at the top of the old Norge, Lana rode the mounting pain and watched for the yellow spots before her eyes to clear as they had many times before. But this time the air bubble wasn't moving. It was stationary and growing. The pain traveled up her raised left arm and up the left side of her neck like poisoned sap. She pulled her elbows slowly down and dug them into her sides. Doubling over into a standing fetal position, she pressed the frog hatchery kit tightly to her chest. As the valves closed, the heart expanded and contracted spasmodically. Lana's knees dropped to the porch floor, the yellow spots before her eyes multiplying like so many amoebae, filling the porch with a sea of yellow. "Frank . . ." There was no response. Her eyes closed. Lana slumped to the porch floor, still clutching the box to her chest.

Frank's thumb cocked the lever and the rewind mechanism on his camera made a whirring sound. He took a fresh roll of film from his shirt pocket and dropped it into the camera. Rising from the picnic table, he lifted the camera to his eye, and turned slowly, finger arched on the shutter release button.

Through the viewfinder lens, Frank's right eye searched the sunporch for Lana. He scanned the room from the right to left, and then left to right, up and down. The camera lens gradually framed Lana's body sprawled on the floor in front of the refrigerator, her floral housedress up past her knees. Frank, less focused than the camera, scrunched his eyes behind the lenses of his glasses and the camera. *What is she up to?* he wondered. Then mind joined eye on the image and Frank came to a vague understanding. The shutter release clicked in response. "Lana!" he called, his voice croaking. "Lana!" The camera dropped, dangling on its strap in front of him.

When the surgeon cut through Lana's breastbone exposing her heart, she didn't flinch. She was far away, standing before a swimming pool at an exclusive resort on a South Pacific island. The pool was built atop a promontory that jutted out over the ocean with a sixty-foot drop from pool to ocean. In her dream, Lana stands on the first of several steep marble steps leading to the pool floor. She wriggles her toes in the water, which seems to have been treated with Ivory Snow detergent. Lana feels self-conscious. Under the bright tropical sun, her thin, diaphanous housedress reveals she is very pregnant at the age of seventy-six. The tanned resort-goers lounging along the pool-side glance at her with feigned nonchalance, then look away in obvious disapproval.

Lana steps further down into the warm, milky water and hears a rumbling behind her. It is the island volcano, its conical peak rising above and beyond the roof of the resort behind her. A reddish-brown plume of ash steadily pours out of its opening, and soon the entire sky is darkened with a reddish-brown fog. The wind picks up, and the people around the pool grab towels and drinks and head for the hotel, their eyes nervously focused on the spouting volcano. Waiters in white jackets hurriedly fold up patio table umbrellas and exit. Lana is alone. Arms at her sides, she dives head first into the warm, sudsy water and glides through it, suddenly aware of, but not surprised by, the baby whale fish talking inside her belly. She knows the time is soon. She surfaces and looks toward the ocean beyond the pool, past the cliff. Six dolphins emerge from the ocean waves, wriggle backwards on their tails in unison, and call out to her in whistles, clicks, and squeaks. She understands that they're calling out to her and her baby to join them in the ocean, yet she can't get from the pool to the ocean. She has lost her arms and legs. Instead she has a wide, gaping mouth, a sleek powerful body, and an anchor-like tail. She resents her swimming-pool confinement. In a display of desperation, she dives the full depth of the pool, shoots back up beyond its surface, and slaps her fanned flukes hard against the water, causing two arched waves to leap from the pool. She repeats this display again and again as the dolphin calls become louder and quicker. Lana the whale becomes more frantic with each repeated dive. Time is running out. She must return to the ocean. The rumbling builds toward her like a travelling drum roll. Booming thunder and the volcano erupts in an explosion of hot lava, ash and rocks, shaking the earth beneath her and cracking open one entire side of the pool, the side facing the ocean below. A cascade of pool water gushes out from the gaping cliff to the ocean, carrying Lana and the baby she is birthing with it. The dolphins join Lana as she begins to ride the ocean waves, finally free, gliding through the water. She turns to see her new baby whale, connected only by the umbilical cord that pulls against her forward movement. Something is very wrong. She whips her body 180 degrees. She whips it again, and then again until the cord detaches. But the baby does not follow. The baby does not search for Lana's milk.

Lana knows. She understands but stays awhile anyway, swimming wide circles on the surface, then re-submerging. The baby does not follow Lana. The ocean is gently sweeping, sweeping Lana's baby away from her. Lana continues circling in the same spot on into the night. It is a dark, deep ocean. It is nighttime now, and the stars are out, and the dolphins silently slip away. The water is dark and deep and cold. Nature finally tells Lana it's O.K. to break the circular pattern, and she heads out into the ocean, searching for warmer waters.

DEKE AND LYDIA

Debra Shore

The trailers lay like metal cartridges flung out on the gravel. The blue lights of TV shone from most. From Lydia's, there was a softer, yellow light. Deke parked his truck behind her MG, walked to the door and up the wooden steps. Looking in the window, Deke saw Lydia's head tucked in to her chest and a book open on her lap. She was asleep.

Deke wanted to turn off the light, to cover her, to carry her to her bed and gently lay her down. His right hand had lifted up as if to touch her in her sleep, to smooth her hair, to rest upon her cheek. He had no license to touch or to be gentle; only with one's children or spouse, none others are granted. As the Sheriff of Pagosa Springs, his mission was to protect, he thought, but was that what this ache was about? To protect Lydia?

He stood alone in the chill of the passing night, looking in on Lydia. One could do far worse in life, he thought, than look in on Lydia.

Quietly, he stepped down backwards and walked to his pickup. He climbed back in, rolled back in neutral for a few paces, then started the motor and drove away.

Fifteen minutes later he was back at Lydia's. Deke felt gripped by her, and he knew now that the symptoms were beginning to show. Chronic diseases surge and subside, and who knows whether the body or the disease, at any given moment, is in control? He knew now that *she* was the driver here, despite his position behind the wheel.

He walked again to her lighted door, again mounted the wooden stairs and looked in.

She was gone. The same light shone. The book lay closed on the couch. But he saw no sign of Lydia.

Deke felt the chill air in his nostrils as he breathed, saw the air in puffs before him as he exhaled. From a nearby trailer he heard the pitch for Hamburger Helper. He knocked on the door.

In a moment he saw her come out from the rear of the trailer. Her face looked scrubbed, and she was snapping up a Western blouse. 'Oh,' he thought, 'don't, please. *I* want to do that. *I* want to touch you there, snap closed that blouse, open up that door at the base of your neck. Let *me* do it, *please.*'

Instead, he said, "Hello, Lydia," when she opened the door. He doffed his hat and smiled widely. "I was passing by and saw the light on. I figured you might want to go to the dance."

"Come on in, Sheriff," she said breezily, sweeping the hair off her neck with one hand and opening the door with the other. "I don't know that I find your story entirely credible, that you were just passing by, but it doesn't entirely matter now, does it?" She grinned at him.

Drawing closer as he entered, he saw a sweep of freckles across her chest in the open V of her blouse. They looked like crumbs to lap up, like sunspots to warm his cheek.

Deke smelled hand lotion, Pine Sol, mint tea. When she shut the door behind him, he heard his heart banging insistently, as if to be let out. Lydia's place was quiet. No TV promoting nonsense. No radio intruding. That set her apart right off, he realized. *She* was quiet.

Lydia noticed his darkened collar and armpits, the fresh bruise of sweat on the brow of his hat.

"Been dancing already, Sheriff?" she asked in an amused tone. "I wouldn't imagine you'd be lacking for dancing partners."

Deke blushed.

She appeared to have just washed her face. A wet ringlet stuck to her neck below her ear. He felt drawn to the expanse of her cheek as a spoon, irresistibly, to a mound of fresh whipped cream. How to get that into his mouth!

"I *have* been dancing," he said suddenly, forcefully, "and I was thinking all the while that it was a downright tragedy that you weren't there having fun too."

Lydia gestured for him to sit down and turned toward the sink.

"I'm sorry you were disappointed, Sheriff, but it is no tragedy, let me assure you. Want some coffee, or a beer?"

Deke felt like a student who had been corrected. Dare he ask her what *is* tragic in this world? Uncork *his* sorrows and seek to pour her own? What bitter drinks would lie before them then?

He let it pass. "Well, maybe not tragic," he said, "I forgot I was speaking to a real literary person, now. What I mean is, I was hoping you'd come to the dance. And when I didn't see you there, I figured maybe you'd like a ride, or needed a nudge, or I could downright drag you off if I acted friendly enough."

Deke looked at her with a winning grin and shrugged.

"And if you say 'No'," he said, "I'm prepared to follow up with an offer of rhubarb pie."

Lydia had spent her life erecting walls, being aloof. She had run away from the university seeking solitude and space. Yet Deke, all shambling and friendly, was penetrating her cloister. She felt irritated, and amused. 'Wait 'til you find out I have nothing to offer,' she thought. 'Claire has my heart.' Claire, her only love, who had left her abruptly months ago and sent her reeling.

"Look at it this way," he said. "The least you can do is have fun. And the rhubarb pie will transport you halfway to heaven, I guar-an-tee it. Looks to me like you're all set to go anyway."

"Deke Cartwright," Lydia said with mock exasperation, "do people here vote for you 'cause they like you, or just to get you to leave them alone?"

"Why, Professor," Deke shrugged, "I reckon as how I can't really say why folks vote for me. I prefer to think it's because I do a good job."

"I see, Sheriff, I see. And I suppose your job for the evening is to escort me to the square dance, is that it?"

"Yes, ma'am, something like that. Yes, I'd say so."

Deke took off his hat and twirled it round in his hands. His hair looked hot and curly.

"All right then, Sheriff. I'm not saying I'll *dance,* now," Lydia said, "but I wouldn't want to keep you from your appointed rounds. Let me get my coat."

She disappeared into the back of the trailer.

At the dance, Deke got Lydia a Coke and leaned close to her ear, explaining the various steps. He nodded and waved to those passing by and introduced Lydia whenever someone stopped. When he could, he mopped his forehead and neck. The room was very hot.

"So there you are," Lorene Blaylock barked out at Deke. "I was wondering where you got off to. Have you recollected left and right, Sheriff, or do you need some additional tutoring?" Deke cringed. Lorene was nothing but a friendly woman, but Lydia didn't know that. He didn't know how solicitous to be. But then Lydia pushed him on the elbow, saying "Go on, Sheriff, I'd like to see you dance. That's why you brought me here, isn't it?" He could've sworn she winked at him. He felt funny about it, but he let Lorene pull him into a square.

In an instant he was caught up in the swirl. Like banjo music, like homemade ice cream, square dancing was a matter of pure pleasure and brought an automatic smile to his face. In the smooth execution of difficult steps, he felt little explosions of joy. He was one part, moving in and out, separating, spinning, making a whole. It gave men and women a chance to be close without being awkward, to clutch and hug and pass through each other's arms on the way to a new configuration.

Lydia saw a man at ease with himself, with his size and grace, with his sex and his humor. The music seeped around her and thrummed along her veins. She heard a voice at her side.

"It's pretty much fun, ain't it?" A tall, lanky cowboy stood next to her looking at the crowd. "Think you might want to give it a whirl?" he said. "I'm Kirk Douglas, by the way," he said turning halfway to her, "and I reckon I've heard just about every response to that you can expect to hear, exceptin' 'Hello, It's a pleasure to meet you.'" He turned to Lydia and extended his hand.

She was shocked by his diffidence and the creases in his face. "Hello," she said, shaking his hand, "it's a pleasure to meet you."

"I'm sorry if this disappoints you, Mr. Douglas," she said, "but I don't know how to dance. I haven't actually done this sort of thing in years. I'd really rather just watch if you don't mind." She found herself searching the crowd for Deke.

"You know with all this racket, I didn't catch your name," she heard him say.

Embarrassed, she turned to him and said, "I'm sorry. It's Lydia. Lydia Passamini."

She realized he had the greenest eyes she had ever seen—pine-green.

Without meaning to, she let herself be led onto the dance floor. Douglas gathered a square about them in no time, and with a combination of gentle pressure on her elbow and whispered directions in her ear, he guided her through the dance. Without meaning to, really, without knowing how or why or exactly even when, Lydia let go. She swirled. She twirled. She do-si-doed. She swung her partner and was swung in kind. She stepped to the center, she went under an arch, she flew around and came back home. She paraded left.

And without meaning to, really, without recognizing that it belonged to her and that she alone could release it, Lydia Passamini laughed.

Propelled into partnership, Lydia discovered that this Kirk Douglas was nothing but bones wrapped in denim. Lydia wondered how something so angular could also glide, and yet glide he did—smoothly, flowingly, without ceasing. There was a joy to it that had somehow escaped Lydia in her fourth-grade phys ed square-dance class. Now her 'whoops' came out as naturally, as uncontrollably, as hiccups.

Lydia's joy, while private, was also infectious. The men in her square felt lifted, stirred. They grasped their partners more warmly, smiled more broadly, relaxed and felt inexplicably dizzy.

Dancing on Lydia's right, Earl Buckelew felt a yearning for sex seize him, sex when he was fresh and young and reckless and quick. Earl swung his wife, twirled her extra pounds and imagined her flabby thighs soft on the inside from rubbing against each other.

Ray Flores, opposite Lydia, felt his penis stir toward her as she passed him on a turn. The arch of her neck, the swirl of her hair, touched him in a forgotten young spot. She made him hopeful and embarrassed and exhilarated all at once.

Ron Barfield, the fourth man in their square, danced better than ever, showing off.

And the wives knew. They could sense the stirring and preening, saw their men looking at Lydia, heard her cascading laugh and felt her unacknowledged power. They knew. They knew, and their eyes sparkled dark with bitterness and remembered lust.

Lydia felt the surge and stir, felt the men brush against her unconsciously, needing to touch. She sensed the electric charge of sex in the air.

'Go to her,' she wanted to say, to Earl Buckelew, to Ray, to Ron, directing them to their wives. 'Go to her, go past the extra pounds, past the neck wattles, past the bags and droops and hard years, go to her breasts swaying under her dress and go to her softest inner thighs and go to the part that welcomes you home, go to the sweet part, the old part, the one clear remembered soft part, and take her there and give it to her. Take your restlessness, take your need, take your yearning and bring it back home, to the sweet home, to the inside home,' she thought. 'I don't need it, I don't want it. Give it back to them,' she thought, 'please, give it to *them*.'

But how could she tell this to Ron, to Ray, to Earl? How could she deflect their fantasies, their rising cocks? This was her dream only, perhaps. She wished she had the power to redirect their desires, but she did not. And they resented her for it, begrudged her ability to inject urgency into their jeans, resented their shackled state and her freedom.

The dance ended. With a flourish and a bow, Douglas escorted Lydia to the sidelines. He smiled at her but seemed unable to express himself when standing still.

"Would you like some soda pop or beer?" he asked.

"No, thank you," Lydia said.

They stood for a few moments in awkward silence. Lydia had no small talk at her disposal. The rest of the crowd milled about talking and drinking and fanning their faces and necks.

Just then Deke sauntered up, mopping his brow.

"Excuse me, Professor," he said leaning in toward her, "but it looks to me like we both have a credibility problem here. I thought you said you couldn't dance." Deke tapped the toe of his right boot on the floor and wagged an index finger at her.

Lydia smiled and blushed. She turned to Kirk Douglas, who stood stone-faced next to them, and gestured warmly. "Why, I had a good teacher, Sheriff. Mr. Douglas here was gracious enough to keep me from embarrassing myself publicly out there. I am in his debt."

"Kirk's one of the best, that's for sure," Deke said. "It don't seem like it when you look at him, but when he starts moving, there's nothing that's smoother, I tell you, and I'm including whipped butter and cream."

Douglas smiled faintly, tipped his hat to them both, and excused himself to get a drink.

Deke whispered in Lydia's ear. "The saddest fellow. Can't talk to women worth a damn, but he's the best dancer you'll see here. It's just him and six hundred head of cattle out on a big spread toward Tres Piedras. Raised his son all by himself. Now the boy's gone off to college. You'll see Kirk at the dances and at church and that's the truth of it."

"What happened to the boy's mother?" Lydia asked. "His wife?"

Deke shook his head sadly. "Got kilt. It's the worst story. Tractor fell over on her. It had been raining and they got a call that a neighbor needed help. She headed out—it was late, you know—and they figured she hit a draw that was slick. Took a while to find her. Seems like Kirk's lost his ability to be with anybody since that."

They paused, each lost to imagining.

'We appear to be human beings,' Lydia thought, 'all carrying our pouches of tragedy and pain, but better to regard ourselves as geologic structures, our faces lined with superficial evidence of huge faults below, the cosmic indifference of the universe visited upon each of us without justice or warning.' Lydia imagined Claire's body crushed under a tractor, her blond hair haloed around her unharmed face. The pain of losing Claire ripped her again.

"I'm parched," Deke said. "Wanna drink?"

Then he saw Lydia's contorted face.

"Are you all right?" Deke asked urgently. "What happened? Was it about Kirk, what I told you about Kirk?"

Lydia nodded silently, afraid to speak, afraid of the tears welling up. She bowed her head and covered her brow with one hand.

"Take me home, Deke," she said in a small voice. "Can you take me home?"

"Sure," he said, "sure, whatever you want." He put his hand on her back and steered her toward his pickup.

He had seen her dancing, had seen delight dust her and linger for a moment on her arms and feet, and now she seemed to have travelled to an unbridgeable sadness.

They drove in silence. Lydia kept her hand to her brow as if to ward off the light. Deke thought she might be crying.

He pulled up to Lydia's trailer and killed the engine. Instantly the sky's enormous silence and pulsing stars pressed upon them. Lydia stuck her head out the truck window as if to let the cool air rain down on her face.

Deke leaned his head back and closed his eyes. The flickering images on the inside of his lids were no match for his dreams, waking and sleeping.

He imagined holding Lydia's hand in the nighttime quiet—two silences joined by thin skin. He imagined stroking her arms, kissing her neck, massaging her back, dancing with her—alone.

GETTING AWAY WITH IT

Dan Peluso

Uncle Benny fell out of a seventh-story window and broke both of his wrists trying to break the fall. I think he was trying to kill himself, really. The thing was, he wasn't telling anyone in our family exactly how he fell out the window, so I think everyone just assumed he wasn't watching where he was going. Anyway, no one really liked Uncle Benny that much. My mother couldn't stand the way he smelled (like mildew, she always said), and he gave my sister the creeps. The way he looked like he was out of his mind all the time really bugged her. He had a big beard, and he was always wearing some kind of turtleneck sweater that looked like it was choking him to death. He didn't want much from life. He just wanted to play his drums and listen to his music.

The time he came to stay with us after he was in the hospital, he really did a number on my poor mother. He said he had to keep doing things with his hands to help them heal from the fall he had. He said that drumming was too hard on them, so he took up painting these ceramic chess pieces until he could start drumming again. It was something to kept his hands working I guess. I always wondered what kind of people spend their time painting those chess pieces whenever I play chess, and now I know it's people like Uncle Benny. So one day he set all his paint and crap up right on our kitchen table after everyone had left the house in the morning. I came home from fishing and brought my rod and reel upstairs to my room. He had about two hundred of these little half-painted knights and things all over the table. He wasn't using any newspaper on the table and there were paint splotches all over my mother's poor kitchen table. I knew she was going to have a fit when she saw this, and I thought I should have told Uncle Benny to have this cleaned up before she got home. I really couldn't though. I mean this guy was supposed to be my uncle and everything. It ended up just like I thought it would. My mother came home and saw my uncle and his big mess and almost wanted to kill him. So my uncle went on with this whole thing about the paint being water-based and being able to wash off with water. Then my mother saw the dog with this chicken bone in his mouth. I didn't even see it until she started screaming.

"The thing's gonna choke on this!" she hollered. It was funny the way she called the dog "thing" like that. If she really cared for it, she wouldn't think of the dog as a *thing*. My uncle got all upset when my mother started hollering and put his brush down in the glass he had filled with water. It took him about a million years to do this because his hands were really messed up like I told you. He looked like how the elephant man would do something. It wasn't funny at all though.

"Hey man, I juss give the dog a bone after I eat my chicken," Uncle Benny said. "Why waiss a good bone like that?"

"That kind of bone breaks off in little splinters the dog can choke on," said my mother. "Don't you know anything!" All of a sudden she was talking like she was an expert on dogs and everything. It was funny. This was the same woman that would sidestep an empty dog dish for weeks, and let the dog go hungry.

"All right now, let's not get all uncool," said my uncle as he started walking towards the dog. He was moving like some kind of old man would. "I'll juss get the bone from the dog and wipe up the table and the place be all yours again."

Under her breath my mother said something like *"It was my house to begin with,"* but I guess my uncle didn't hear it. He never hears anything personal about himself that people say. Otherwise he might just get those stupid ponytails cut out of his hair. Oh yeah, didn't I tell you about all the little ponytails he has in his hair? He has about twenty little ponytails in the back of his hair, tied up with those little garbage bag ties. You know the things with the little metal wire in them? It's the most disgusting thing in the world to look at all those things in his hair. But he must like it or something. He doesn't even take them out to wash his hair ever. Anyway, it got to be a real big argument between the two of them, and I made off to my room before I saw something really bad happen.

From my room I could hear my mother hollering at Uncle Benny. She was really giving it to him, too. It was a good thing my sister wasn't home because she always likes to take sides with my mother whenever she's yelling at someone. It's really sad when my mother is yelling at the dog for chewing up a shoe or something, and my sister will come from somewhere to help my mother give the poor dog hell. I tried to do something in my room that would tune out what was going on in the living room, but it's really hard not to listen in on a good argument.

"I want you outta here!" my mother screamed. "You don't do a damn thing, and you expect me to cater to you hand and foot because you have no place else to go. How old are you now, Ben? You're not a kid anymore. It's time to start fending for yourself!"

"Yeah, yeah," I heard my uncle say. "I'm tryin' to get my act together. Juss be a little more time and I can get these doorknobs of hands I got here to work gigs for me again."

"I don't care what you've gotta do," said my mother. "Just get the hell out of here." She sounded like she was calming down a little bit. She wears out after a while.

Uncle Benny argued with my mother some more, then he came into my room because that was where he kept his clothing bag and immediately went rooting through the bag looking for something. I pretended not to notice because I didn't want to get into any kind of conversation with him. I know after I've been yelled at by somebody, the last thing I want is someone talking to me. Anyway, I saw him pull out his little bag with white stuff in it. I wondered if it was sugar or something but I was only fooling myself. Uncle Benny used to be into drugs a long time ago, and I guess he started it up all over again. Maybe it was just when he got depressed about something he did it, I don't know. He took the bag into the bathroom and closed the door. It gave me enough time to go looking through his bag for a while. I don't know what I was looking for, really, all of a sudden I just felt like one of those P.I.'s from the cop shows on TV, like Magnum or something. I didn't find much in there, just some of his rotten old clothes and a pair of socks. I heard the bathroom door start to open. For a minute I had forgotten that I was rooting through someone else's stuff and didn't act quick enough. Uncle Benny came into my room and saw me with my paws digging around in his bag.

"What the hell, man," he said as he fished around in his pocket. "Looking for something?"

I really didn't know what to say to him. I didn't want him to know that I was looking for drugs or anything. "I thought the dog's bone might have fallen in here," I said to him. It was probably the lamest thing I could have thought of, but it was better than telling him I was from the drug squad or something.

"I think we need to establish juss whose stuff is whose around here," he said to me very seriously. "I can't have people rooting through my stuff like that. That cool with you?"

I don't think I ever saw him so angry before. He must really have had something to hide from me. I told him maybe he should keep his stuff somewhere else if he wanted more privacy. If he was going to keep his bag in *my* room, I might accidentally look in there once in a while. He didn't seem too happy with the way I said things to him, but if I told him I knew what was going on, I think he would have really had something to be mad about. Anyway, just when I thought the whole thing was over, my mother came in the room and saw that me and Uncle Benny were having some words. She wanted to know what was going on, and Uncle Benny said that he found me rooting through his stuff. My mother took an offense and asked me what I was doing. Here's where I really blew it.

"I thought I saw him with something," I said.

"What?" my mother asked.

"A dog bone," my uncle interrupted. I knew he was doing that to get me off the real reason I was looking through his bag, which I think he knew by then.

"Why did you look in there for a dog bone?" my mother asked. She had this look on her face like things weren't clear to her.

"Never mind," I said. "I won't look through there any more. O.K.?"

"No," my mother said. "It's not O.K. I want to know what you were doing in the bag."

"It's really O.K., Fred," Uncle Benny said to my mother. I knew she hated being called Fred like that. Her name was Freddy. It was kind of a man's name and everything, but you get used to it being your mother's name after a while. "The kid was looking for a dog bone. *That's all.*"

Then, all of a sudden, I turned stupid and said, "No I wasn't. Uncle's hiding something in there."

There was too much silence in the room after I said that. I knew my uncle was wondering what would happen if we found that bag he had in his pocket. He's been borrowing my father's money for the past ten years to support his drug habit. That would really make my father happy when he got home that day. To find out he wasn't helping a starving artist with his art, but with his addiction. Uncle Benny admitted to my mother what he was hiding in the bag; he knew we would find out sooner or later, I guess. He begged for us not to tell my father about it, but my mother was just too upset about the whole thing. I can't remember everything that happened here exactly the way it happened, but I do remember wondering if then would have been a good time to tell my family about me flunking English class and not really graduating from high school. I mean after my father got home and heard about what Uncle Benny did with all the money he's been getting. Sometimes when someone else is in trouble, it's a good time to be in trouble because you're not the only one in trouble. It probably wouldn't have been good for me to talk about flunking English, because even before my father got home, my mother and uncle sat down for the longest conversation in the world, right at the living room table where all Uncle Benny's mess was. They talked all about how terrible this habit of my uncle's was and everything, and how much money it had been costing him. He didn't say anything about paying back the eight thousand or so that he owed my father. According to him he wasn't even a drug addict or anything, he was just a casual user of cocaine and crack once in a while.

"I can't believe you've been hiding this from us all these years," my mother said to Uncle Benny. "I feel like a damn fool!"

"Hey man," said my uncle, "it's a tough world out there in the music business. Everybody's doing the stuff."

"Oh my God! That's not an excuse, Benny," said my Mother. "You can't use your job as a crutch. Look at my husband. He works ten hours a day in front of computers for a living—he's stayed clean."

"It's different," said Uncle Benny. "I've got to be able to create. Sometimes I need a little lift, that's all. Juss a couple of hits before a gig and I'm set."

"How many is *a couple?*" asked my mother.

"It depends on the crowd, the music, and my mood," he answered.

"So if you're in a good mood you don't have to call my husband up for money, is that it?" asked my mother.

"Why do we have to make an issue out of this?" asked my uncle. "Why do we have to make this public with the family?"

"Because it's been the family's money that you have been pissing away," said my mother. She got up from the table and went into the kitchen. When my father's car pulled into the driveway the dog started barking and smacked its head into the wall because it couldn't see where it was going that well. I wondered what more could have gone wrong that day with this family?

THE MORNING ROUTINE

Ann Langlais

Fourteen-year-old Grace sat on the toilet with her canary-yellow robe bunched around the top of her thin thighs. As she rubbed, in small circles with her fingertips, a mint cleansing mask to her face, her eyes wandered to her naked father who, with legs spread and face plastered with shaving cream, leaned into the steamy mirror, contemplating where to plant the next stroke of his razor blade. Usually, when she shared the bathroom with her father in the morning, Grace felt half-asleep, mesmerized by the warm glow of the bathroom's red velvet wallpaper, except when her father (a wildly moody and unpredictable man) would abruptly lunge for a toothbrush, or spin around to the towel rack. Then his nakedness came at her all too quickly and she flinched, sometimes grabbing the ruffles at the collar of her soft, canary-yellow robe.

Grace screwed the lid back on her jar of cleansing mask, then wiped her hands on a wet face cloth. It concerned her: Would she have enough time for her whole morning routine before catching the bus to school? She began mentally calculating the time for each step of her beauty routine but then gave up because she knew there was no way she would skip over a step, for it made her nervous, panicked, to not feel she was looking her prettiest. Nor could she get ready in a rush, like the girls who jumped, out of breath, haphazardly, onto the school bus, then came down the aisle shaking their wet hair and chewing a cold piece of toast. No! Grace stiffened at the thought, her fingertips still pressed to her temples. Girls like that who ate chocolate and scribbled messily in their notebooks, and who could be so flirtatious with life, danced, in quick movements, strictly on the periphery of Grace McKlennon's life, sometimes mocking her, she felt. But then again, their future did not rest like Grace's in the physical shape she inhabited. As it was written in the approving expressions of those around her—her dance instructors, her brothers, her parents, her friends—that from Grace McKlennon, nothing less than a perfectly thin and vibrant body could come, after each *fouette,* bounding into the dance studio mirror.

She continued in her daydream for a moment, then found her eyes had settled on her father's cock.

She found his cock strangely horrifying, yet exciting at the same time. It was so big and of such a strange texture, and it hung there so effortlessly with an end that weirdly mushroomed. And he seemed so unaware of it! But instead went on shaving, his legs spread, his feet flat on the bath mat, the marbled sink top bumping him at the top of his pubic hair. He shaved with his elbow high in the air, his head tilted back, and as he brought the blade up his neck through the thick shaving cream (Grace McKlennon's father had a very coarse beard), everything seemed to pull with the gesture, including his genitals which bounced upward ever so slightly.

And here Grace was sure she felt a rhythm emerging from the repeated upward motions of his hand, body, and cock (after all, dancers know rhythms!). And feeling the rhythm, she looked with deep pleasure into her mind's eye and saw herself dancing across the ballet studio floor into the stained glass window's streams of violet and blue light.

But now joining the rhythm was a whistle, a beautiful whistle with swirls in it, bird-like, but with a deeper melody, and, again, Grace danced across the floor, the whistle now releasing her body to bend and arc, to turn, to flow! Where was this sound coming from? She let go of the fantasy, which quickly dissolved, and looked over at her father. She had never heard him whistle like that! Not like that! Usually, he was so difficult, downright ugly at times! Can he see into my mind? she thought. And keeping her eyes on her father, she pulled on the roll of toilet paper, listening to him whistle, and thinking of how perfectly, how sweetly the melody accompanied her dance, as if he did know what yearned in her heart!

Grace slipped off the toilet and flushed it. She stepped behind her father to the built-in shelves at one end of the bathtub and gathered her toothbrush, shampoo, and soap. She lined each item up along the edge of the bathtub while looking over her shoulder at her father, her glance catching on his naked butt. She waited for his whistling to end, then for him to wipe the last traces of shaving cream off his face, and drop the wash cloth into the laundry hamper. He then studied his face in the mirror and cleaned the corners of his eyes with a Q-Tip while Grace observed that even though her father appeared to be in such a good mood, something still brooded beneath his thick, fleshy eyelids (the same heavy eyelids inherited by all the McKlennon children). Finally, with her pale green face rising into the mirror beside him, she asked, "Dad? You know the father/daughter dinner dance is at the end of this month?"

"You don't say . . . " he said, hearing only some childish chattering at the tip of his elbow, which jutted out while he clipped his nose hairs. And please don't bump my arm, he thought. He started whistling again, reaffirming that he really was in a good mood that morning. He felt quite invincible, in fact. And how exhilarating it was to finally feel alive again! How it pained him that no matter how hard he tried sometimes life left him utterly and hopelessly depressed. And sometimes days—months—were lost as he tried to carry on in a black and heavy fog. He stopped clipping and turned his head from side to side, looking for more nose hairs to cut.

"So are we going?"

"Going?" He looked at his daughter—what was she talking about?

"To the father/daughter dinner dance?" she repeated. He stared at her, the strange goop on her face, her robe, the part in her hair, while it all dawned on him, she was asking him to a dance. And isn't this what he had been waiting for? Had he not spent years, with Mrs. McKlennon helping by giving Grace a Valium, or a Librium, slipping into her bedroom at night, touching her, preparing her so one day she would be ready. How he believed in physical love in the family! The warmth of his children always helped him through his darkest hour. Yet, when the voice of God spoke to the good doctor for a short time, the doctor might purge himself of his ways. But no matter how hard he tried, some seductive force, some force that he could not be expected to control, always came to pull at him when he was his most depressed.

"Dad? Did you want to go?"

"Yes, Gracie, I would love to go. I just can't believe how much you've grown up and right before my very eyes!" He held her arms out at her sides and planted a kiss on her head. Grace giggled. It was like some kind of dream, her father in such a good mood, and the way he knew the melody to her fantasy ballet, and now all her friends would see them together at the school dance! She leaned forward to hug him, but then glancing down at his cock, she stepped back and giggled. Giggled!? She turned away, and drew the shower curtain in front of the tub. What on earth was so funny? she thought. She looked over her shoulder as she unzipped her robe, and saw, in the mirror, that her father was watching her. And, again, she giggled! And everything was suddenly so hilarious, so carefree, like the girls that came rushing late for the bus, that she found herself dropping her robe right in front of her father, not caring if he caught a glimpse of her backside!

And once in the shower, with the water busy cleaning every speck of that crusty mask and other undesirable dirt off her body, another wave of exhilaration came over her which she couldn't wait to share with her father who she knew oddly was still listening. "Daniel is making me a dress that will be perfect."

"He is?" Dr. McKlennon shook his head, for his son, Daniel, never ceased to amaze him. He saw his son busy right and left designing clothes, with girlfriends parading in and out of the house. BUT, the doctor was disappointed to learn, Daniel never went on any dates, nor did he sleep with girls. Dr. McKlennon was completely baffled! It never occurred to the doctor to consider that, truthfully, his son was gay.

"The dress is going to be beautiful, Dad."

"You're going to be beautiful, Gracie . . ." Dr. McKlennon turned toward the shower curtain. If it was the closest thing to his daughter's body right now, he would gladly look at it. And there in the plastic curtain's swirly pearl design, he considered what a miracle it was that he had actually fathered a child, a girl child, that was going to love him back in that special way reserved for lovers, while at the same time giving to him her innocence and her childlike devotion. Yes! It was only a matter of time now before it happened!

"The dress is long and full," Grace continued. "It took yards and yards of fabric, beautiful white fabric with the tiniest pattern on it that looks like rows of golden wheat." She saw again, in her mind, the sketches that Daniel had drawn, but now the sketches in their thin paper and weak pencil came to life, for now she believed that her father, and not just her father, but this gentle and charming man who she shared the bathroom with this morning, would be at her side. Blast it! While washing her face, she got some soap in her eyes! Now . . . where was that towel?

Dr. McKlennon watched as Grace reached, with both her eyes squeezed shut, out from behind the shower curtain and groped along the towel rack. The two soft mounds on her chest, cupcake size and now glistening wet, appeared to be struggling so hard, so intensely, to become full-sized breasts. It was all the doctor could do to keep his hands flat on the countertop, and not rush to her aid and massage them, he felt so committed, so involved, in the peril of those two budding mounds of life. But then a miracle, as today was a day for miracles, a faint breeze crossed his daughter's chest, and her nipples, as if of a separate conscience, became hard, as if to whisper hello to their secret friend, the good doctor.

Grace dried her eyes. Ouch! What a sting! Blinking very hard, she struggled to stretch them open, and stood for a moment, completely oblivious to her father, as the bathroom came back into view. It took a moment for her to register that her father was leaning against the counter, watching her. "Your breasts are developing so nicely, Gracie. I think that you're going to need to start wearing a bra soon!"

"Daddy!" Grace shrieked, covering her body with the shower curtain, "You're not supposed to be looking at me!"

"I'm a doctor, Gracie . . . What do you think, I examine my patients with their clothes on?"

"Well . . . no." She pulled the curtain closed and sealed it with some water she splashed onto the tiled wall. Once back into the warm water showering down, she crossed her arms over her chest and cupped her breasts. It was silly of her to get so embarrassed whenever the subject of bras came up. At school and at the dance studio, she always left her top hanging around her neck while underneath she slipped her leotard on. The truth was she didn't want the other girls to see that while they paraded around in white, black (sometimes red and green!), push-up, underwire, and cross-your-heart bras, she hadn't even begun to wear one. It baffled Grace as to how to give her mother the hint that it was time to take her shopping for one. But now, she thought (and here she busied herself applying a palmful of purple shampoo to her hair) that maybe, like Daniel, it was men who better understood these matters of her feminine image.

"The dress for the dinner dance that I've been telling you about . . . I don't think that I'm going to need a bra under that dress." Grace loosened her hands from her tangled hair and, looking down at them, paused to consider this new direction in their relationship.

"So what is it about this dress that a young lady would not need a bra with it?"

"Well . . . the straps would show!" She giggled, then stopped because she thought her father might think she was laughing at him for concerning himself with her problems. But she could not stop her urge to giggle, so she covered her mouth with her hand and giggled silently to herself. She imagined the giggling to be a natural part of what erupted in intimate talks between mother and daughter. So why not a good giggle between father and daughter? She continued, only talking louder now, for her father was slapping himself with aftershave, "The dress has big, puffy sleeves that are practically at the edge of your shoulder. It's something like what Olivia Hussey wore in 'Romeo and Juliet'."

"Oh, I see, well then you're probably right and you shouldn't wear a bra."

"Yeah, that's what I thought." Grace smiled to herself. She was so satisfied they had even broached the subject of bras, and her father agreed with her decision to go braless under the puffy-sleeved dress (as if she really did know something about bras!), she forgot completely to suggest that he take her shopping for one. No, her mind had already raced on, for there was something else, critical, that she had to ask. "Dad?" Grace began. She heard the tick, tick, tick which meant her father was on the bathroom scale, and for a moment, for every tick, a number flashed before her eyes, a number which represented fat, fat that was on her body, fat that was her butt and her thighs . . . . She tensed her back and bit her lip. It was insane that she ask this question for if the answer came out wrong, surely she would die!

"Yes, Grace, were you saying something?"

"I . . . I . . ." She had to know, and when else could she ask, so she put down her hair conditioner as if to lighten her perilous flight. "A lot of people have said that I remind them of Olivia Hussey. Do you think I'm as pretty as her?" Grace shrank back as if her question had immediately consumed a large portion of the room. Then when her father did not answer right away, she thrust her chest directly in line with the shower's hard pelts, letting it all come down hard on her and reddening her skin, for it was a stupid question anyway.

Dr. McKlennon was, without warning, now hopelessly lost. He stared into the open medicine cabinet, his thumbs dug into the fleshy part on the back of his hips. The doctor reached out and turned the vials that lined the medicine cabinet one more time to check the prescription labels, for he sensed something was missing: Placidyl, Valium, Lotusate, Dexedrine, Didrex, Tenuate, Pondimin, Ritalin. His eyes followed each vial as it turned from the white label to reveal the colored pills it contained. Yellow, orange, red, white. In all of medical science, at that time, no one knew how to help the poor doctor with his terrible moods. So he doctored himself with his collection of pills, and sometimes felt like God, when in a wave of a hand over his mouth, if he was feeling too happy, he could feel sad. Or, if he was moving too slowly, he could speed himself up. But sometimes terrible complications set in, and most of the time, Dr. McKlennon hated to admit, the pills had no real power—like expecting a paper cup to battle its way against the current of a dark and turbulent sea.

Moments ago, when Dr. McKlennon first opened the cabinet, he had simply been curious to take stock. But now that he was certain a vial was missing, the whole collection seemed dismally, fatally, incomplete. He faced the open cabinet and, without his moving enough for it be noticed, he collapsed inside as violently as a building, after the white flash of an atom bomb, implodes in a cloud of dust to the street, vaporizing with it floors of office people into oblivion and dust. As it always was, there was hardly a perceptible movement to his body as the good doctor imploded inside. His shoulders slumped, his chin loosened and sank, slowly into his neck.

But even in his barely perceptible transformation, it only took one glance outside the shower curtain at his curled hair on the silent back of his head for Grace McKlennon to know her father was undergoing a drastic change. "Dad?" she said.

The doctor turned around and felt a slow, heavy knock in his heart when he looked at Grace peeking out from the curtain with a head of sweet, soaking hair. Grace, quite ill-prepared as to what to say, could only blurt out her earlier question: "Do you think I'm as pretty as Olivia Hussey?"

The doctor felt another slow, heavy knock in his heart, which reverberated through his entire numb body. His eyes glossed over with tears and wavered over his daughter's forehead. Her question moved him, for it breathed the simple, pleasurable worries of a young girl's life. And simply by being the recipient of such a question, Dr. McKlennon believed he was being granted some time to forget that he was an old man and remember what it was like to be a carefree young man!

"Gracie, you are the most beautiful Juliet of all!" And here the doctor slowly opened the curtain and stepped into the shower. With one hand, he gently caressed Grace's right breast, while, with his other hand, he lifted up her hand where, above her knuckles, he planted a kiss. Grace's only awareness was of the kiss. In later years, she might reconstruct the morning her father kissed her hand as having been a staged joke over breakfast, with her hand stretching across the table over a half-eaten piece of toast. But she did feel the kiss, and concentrated on it, its tender pressure, its even circle of skin. It was like a door in front of a hidden place where her entire body went to. From a point between her shoulder blades, she opened, her whole chest splitting apart, each piece floating away and then being pulled together where they slipped through the door.

Todd, Grace's older brother, kicked open the door. Dr. McKlennon hopped from the shower. Like his father, Todd was completely naked (except for a pair of thong sandles and wire-rimmed glasses), and after shutting the door, he began grabbing at the long, bushy hair on top of his head, sticking out his tongue while he maneuvered his hair into the clutches of a rubber binder. The whole time Todd McKlennon looked right on past his father's perturbed expression, swung wide his feet at the base of the toilet, lifted the lid, and proceeded to urinate. "Man, oh man, that was quite the time last night. You wouldn't believe the chicks, Dad, you just would not believe." Dr. McKlennon slammed closed the medicine cabinet and flung open, to check again, the top sink drawer. Grace peered out at her disheveled brother from behind the curtain while she turned off the shower, wrapped a towel around herself, then struggled with a large comb to untangle her wet hair.

Finished, Todd crossed behind his father to the sink, "Are you looking for your Seconal?"

"What do you know about it?" said Dr. McKlennon. Todd, now drying his hands, indifferently remarked,

"I gave some to a friend last night. He was having trouble coming down."

"You what!" Dr. McKlennon shouted. "Are you crazy? If that kid were to overdose, I could be sued!" He whacked Todd's head. "You idiot!" Todd defiantly shrugged his shoulders. Grace crouched behind the curtain trying to pretend she was not there. Dr. McKlennon slapped Todd's face, a move that Todd somehow did not anticipate, and, visibly shaken, he grabbed for the countertop. "Go upstairs and get it, and if you're not back down here in ten seconds, you'll be sorry that you were ever born!" Dr. McKlennon opened the door and gave him a kick in his Achilles as he ran out.

Dr. McKlennon was so incensed that with his face turning red, his jaw hardening, and his eyes tightening, he forgot about Grace and punched the shower curtain. "Ah!" Grace yelped as her father's punch hit her in the rib cage. Dr. McKlennon yanked back the curtain,

"What are you doing there?" he said abruptly.

"I was combing the snarls out of my hair," Grace said timidly.

"Oh," he said flatly, then turned sharply to the sink and began reparting his hair. Grace stood with her towel wrapped around her, her comb between her hands, at a loss with her father, watching his angry movements as he flicked his hair around his head. Suddenly, she was filled with a profound sadness, and found herself acting on the only question that came to mind. She stepped out of the tub and tapped her father on the shoulder. And, although his eyes burned at her, she asked,

"Did you want to kiss my hand?"

Dr. McKlennon stared at Grace for a moment, then putting his comb down said, "I have to get going. If I don't leave right now, I'm going to be late." Then he threw his robe over his shoulders and left.

Grace climbed up on the bathroom counter and with her feet in the sink, looked at her face in the mirror. Todd came back, this time with a pair of bell bottoms thrown on, and with his friend, a tall guy with a long neck that Grace had never seen before. Startled, she held her towel tight when they walked in. "Where did Dad go?" Todd asked.

"I don't know, he said something about being late."

"What a totally funked-out bathroom," Todd's friend interjected. "I know I must have come in here last night—but I thought I was hallucinating or something."

"Pretty cool," Todd said. "Look, here's my father's collection." He opened the drawer and all the vials came rolling forward.

"Would you look at that stash." Todd was pleased with his friend's ecstatic expression. "It's like Halloween, all year round." Todd's friend looked down into the drawer, rubbing his chin. "It must be great having a doctor as a father."

"Yeah, well . . ."

"Hey, who's the chick?"

"That's my sister, Grace."

"Oh wow man, she's beautiful."

"Oh yeah, hands off." Then grinning at Grace, Todd added, "She's mine."

"You got any more sisters? . . . How many McKlennons are there?" Just then Daniel appeared at the bathroom door, wearing a robe and hair rollers,

"Hey, can I get in here to pee?"

"Is that another sister?" said Todd's friend.

"No! Come on . . . let's go." Daniel closed the door behind him, sat down on the toilet and began removing his nail polish.

"What are you doing up so early?" Grace turned and asked her brother who hardly looked awake.

"MOM is making me go with her to work at the library. Can you believe that? She says, 'If you're not in school, you have to do something.' So she is making me go with her."

"Oh." Grace turned back to the mirror. Just then a loud pounding on the door began. It was Grace's mother.

"All right you two, knock it off and let me in. I have to pee."

"Shhhhhhh . . ." Daniel whispered, but loud enough to irritate his mother. "Be quiet and maybe she'll figure we're all dead and go away or something . . ."

"Very funny!" Mrs. McKlennon boomed from out in the hallway. Daniel got off the toilet and let her in. She was stark naked.

"AHHHH!!!" Daniel very theatrically pantomimed, "It's the creature from the black lagoon!!!" His eyes filled with disgust at the sight of his mother's naked body. Grace looked over and cringed, rolling her bare shoulders forward, but then straightened up for she did not want her mother to see her timidness.

"I'm warning you!" Mrs. McKlennon said very crossly, then sat down on the toilet.

"Daniel," Grace began, "can you braid my hair for me?"

"Do I have to do everything for you, Gracie?"

"Please."

"O.K." He combed her hair back and began braiding, stopping every now and then to whisper in her ear. "Look at Mom! She is so groggy, she probably floated with Lucy through the Diamond Sky last night. She probably doesn't even know what day it is. We should try and convince her it's Sunday, or better yet, it's Christmas or something. There she goes, I think she's falling asleep . . . let's sneak out and lock her in here."

Grace laughed. Like when she was in the shower and giggled with her father, everything was suddenly, mysteriously funny. She looked in the mirror at the rabbit's ears knot in her towel and at the crown of rollers on her brother's head, and laughed. And laughed.

HOW TO GO BAGGIN'

Brett Liljegren

I wish that I could give you some background on the sport of baggin', but there is truly little known about its origin. Some *aficionados* believe that it was inadvertently started by a guy named Elmer in Sheboygan, Wisconsin. It seems Elmer had to take the trash to the curb at the bottom of his steep driveway one slippery winter's morn. He was in a hurry as he saw the garbage truck rumbling down the street and did not heed the slick ice which covered the blacktop or, for that matter, his wife's cautioning from the kitchen window. Losing his footing, he fell on top of a half-full bag but, clutching it tightly with his elbows and knees, managed to ride it to the bottom. Elmer skidded to a stop, laughing gleefully, and was met with a round of applause from the easily astounded garbage men of Sheboygan who urged him to do it again. And not having much to do in Sheboygan during the winter, he did just that, refining it to the form in which it is now practiced. Or something like that. Others claim that it began with some loonie king of Sweden. I myself place more faith in the Elmer Theory. After all, they also go cow-tipping for fun in Sheboygan.

The materials needed for baggin' are quite simple. It is a winter sport, so a good amount of snow is needed. It is all that much better if the snow is of the dry, new-fallen type, the kind that sounds like a box of corn starch being squeezed when you walk on it. And this snow should be on a moonlit hill. And this moonlit hill is optimally located on a golf course, as they tend to offer the fewest obstacles for your flight-path. This factor of location may necessitate some advance scouting, but it shouldn't be all that difficult.

You will need a group of friends crazy enough to join you in this escapade. Baggin' is not a solo sport. You and your friends must gather alcohol for your upcoming adventure. I say alcohol meaning liquor because beer will simply not cut it. The alcohol helps you think you are warm on a cold winter's night, it helps convince you that you may actually be able to go through with all of this, and it also seems to increase the hilarity factor of the whole situation. I myself suggest peppermint schnapps, or I would if I hadn't drunk so much of it the last time I went . . . but that's another story.

The final items you need are actually the most important, and these are the garbage bags, I personally recommend Hefty Two-Ply Steel Sacks for their durability and roominess, but just about any brand could work, provided they are of the tall or long variety.

Now that the necessary supplies have been gathered, you must of course dress for the occasion. Layering is definitely the best way to go. Remember that it is a winter night, so warmth is important, but then again, so is the padding provided by these multiple layers. You will know you are wearing enough when you can't quite lower your arms all the way to your sides. A pair of warm, dry boots is also a good thing to have, as you will have to do some walking in the snow. Top all of this off with a pair of gloves or mittens, and the most outrageous knit hat you can find, and you're ready to go.

Once you reach the pre-scouted location complete with snow, hill, and moon-light, it is time for the ceremonial Donning of the Bag. But do not let the idea of a ceremony scare you, as this is not at all a solemn event. In fact, now would be a good time to begin consuming the alcohol. Once you have wet your whistle, remove one single bag from the box for yourself, then pass the box to your left in the time-honored tradition. Hold it at arms' length by the two corners of the bottom, or the end opposite the opening, to become acquainted with your bag. It may riffle slightly in the chill breeze as if it could barely contain the excitement which it holds for you. You may wish to examine both sides of the bag in an effort to distinguish front from back, but do not worry about it, as there is no such thing as a front or back to a garbage bag. Next, very carefully poke three holes in the bottom of the bag, one at each corner and one in the middle. This will allow an easier time of putting on your bag. To do so, simply slip the bag over your head, going against everything that Mother ever taught you about plastic bags, with arms upright until the bottom of the bag rests on the top of your head. Then gently, so as not to tear the bag un-necessarily, push your head and arms through the pre-started holes. You are now clothed in the manner of the great baggers who came before you, such as Elmer of Sheboygan.

Take a look around at your friends who by now should have completed the same procedure, and just try not to laugh. This is another good time to take a pull off that bottle. And now you are ready to commence baggin'.

Stand at the top of the hill and gaze down the smooth, pristine, white snow broken only by the shadows of trees from the moonlight. The slight breeze will crinkle your bag as it has grown stiff in the cold of the night. Bare your teeth into that breeze as a shiver of excitement runs down your spine. Take another drink, as baring your teeth into a winter breeze and shivering tends to make you cold. Are you ready? Take off at an easy trot that will soon become an out-of-control wind-milling sprint as you are running down the hill. At that point, hurl yourself into space with the most graceful swan dive you can manage. This swan dive, though, is fated to become a bellyflop into the soft blanket of snow, and you're off.

The velocity which you will quickly attain while racing down a snow-covered hill on your stomach wearing a garbage bag will astound you. Yell and laugh as you become a rocket zipping through the frozen night, snow flying up into your face and melting in the tears forced from your eyes by the wind of your flight. You bounce, tumble, and speed down the hill totally out of control. And then, all too quickly, the race slows as you reach the bottom and finally coast to a stop in a breathless heap. You'll not be able to feel your face as you swipe the melting snow out of your eyes. Your heart will be racing from the thrill and your head reeling from the speed, or maybe the alcohol, but I can guarantee that you will want to run to the top of the hill to do it all again.

DIGGING

William Boerman-Cornell

A backhoe is essentially a tractor with a digging tool on the back that works a lot like your arm. Reach your arm out once, palm down. Form your hand into a cup, and then drag it back toward you, letting your fingers bite into the dirt—the way a little kid digs in the sandbox—and you've got the idea of what a backhoe does.

To picture a backhoe, start out thinking of a tractor, the kind they have on the farm. Now attach two scoops. One on the front end that is kind of like a bulldozer, only cupped like a bucket. That bucket will be just perfect if you've got to scrape up some piles of dirt or stone or gravel and dump it in the back of a truck, but if you want a hole dug, this thing is too clumsy.

Now go round to its backside and attach a hoe. This is the part that digs like a little kid. It looks like a scorpion's stinger, cocked high above the body of the machine, ready to stab down into the earth.

You'll want to put a swivel on the seat so the operator can drive the thing to where he wants it, then swivel the seat around and look out the back end to see what he's doing. Using the set of pedals and levers that he can reach from his new seat position, the operator can uncurl the hoe and start working. The range of digging options open to him is limitless. With the power at his fingertips, the operator can curl the bucket in and stretch it out, he can raise, lower, swing right or left, dig, dump, push, and—in short—accomplish everything the kid in the sandbox can, only on a far grander scale.

All of this is possible only through a hydraulic pump located in the engine compartment and a twisted mass of hydraulic cables which provide power to each independent hinge and swivel of the arm. The intricate pathways that the hydraulic fluid follows from the engine compartment pump, in precise imitation of the blood in a body pumped by the heart, are a collective wonder so amazing that to attempt to describe the specifics of its workings here would only serve to distract the reader from the natural poetry of the backhoe in motion.

I concede, this ballet of movement is not always obvious. You're in a hurry to get somewhere, and there's this whole line of cars backed up behind an ungainly backhoe bouncing along at forty-five with flashing yellow lights and a hoe on its backside. On such occasions, the backhoe is like a penguin on land, waddling slowly to where it has to go. You may, at times like this, become so irritated that, as you pass, you signal your displeasure to the driver of the backhoe by means of a gesture which leaves no question about your feelings.

But restrain that finger a moment. Consider the last time you saw one tearing up a single lane of the road, arm reaching into a deep hole, and bucket coming up with dirt, then swiveling and dumping it on the sidewalk. Remember your rapt amazement at the operator's cybernetic magic, and ask yourself if there could ever be a sight as inspiring or breathtaking. As one who has crossed the globe in search of a more poetic unity of man and machine, I can only confirm that a man and his backhoe are nothing short of the ultimate art form.

About a year ago, Frog and I got this job to hand-dig our way down to a storm pipe. We figured it would be an easy enough job. Routine, anyhow. A leak in a storm sewer about ten feet down had eroded the sand around it and created a cavity, which later collapsed and became a sink hole. You get these all the time on your residential streets. They start out as a little bump, then a hole, then, next thing you know they're swallowing cars.

Thing is, this one wasn't in the road, it was in the middle of a parkway, you know, them strips of grass, halfway between the curb and the sidewalk. This particular strip of grass was pretty thin, so we couldn't get a backhoe in there.

Our problem was, if we set the backhoe up in the street, there wouldn't be enough space between the walk and the curb to get the bucket down into the dirt. The only way we'd have enough room would be to pull the backhoe onto the driveway next to the parkway, but it was a single layer of crumbly asphalt, and the boss decided that just getting a backhoe near that driveway would cause it to crumble, and he didn't feel like paying to repave it. Besides, what boss gives a rip if the grunt labor lives or dies?

So me and Frog had to do it by hand.

The first five feet went slick as a greased slug. There was room for both of us to work, and we dug fast, alternating turns as we pitched out the sand onto a pile on the other side of the walk. Frog liked to pull up with his wrist just before he let a shovelful of sand go. That would make the shovelful hold its shape, but rotate end over end in the air before crashing into the pile.

The nice thing about that job was that there were women coming into and going out of these apartment houses around us all day long. Some of them were sunbathing on their decks, so we had plenty to talk about.

Frog whistled low and said, "The one in the blue tank top is mine." She had brown hair and eyes and "What a body."

"You already got a girlfriend."

Frog laughed, "What she don't know ain't gonna hurt her."

"I got the one in yellow."

"No way. She's a cow."

I didn't hear him, though. I was just staring. Frog whistled and she turned and flipped her hair and smiled. After that, I just glowed.

We kept working at the same time though. Some bosses say you ought to shut up when you work, but talking helps pass the time, and like Frog always says, "Can't work a mean goat hard as a happy one."

About five feet down, we had to start angling the walls of the hole inward, to cut down on the chance of a cave-in. So it would be first Frog down there, then he would jump up, grab my hand, and boost himself out, and I would go down and dig some more. Since it was too deep to throw the dirt out, the guy who wasn't digging would haul the dirt up in a five gallon bucket with a rope tied to the handle. It was when I was down there, running close to nine feet deep, that I hit the pipe. I could feel the shock run through the shovel. I called up to Frog that I figured it would only be ten or so more buckets before we'd be ready to patch.

He was hauling the bucket up when a side caved in. I remember I'd just been noticing how cool it was down there, and thinking how lucky I was to be out of the sun, when the side flowed down like a wave. The whole bank slid, but it was nearly silent. Only a whisper of dirt as the avalanche hit bottom in a second and the sand stacked up against my body all the way to my mouth.

The force of it slammed me against the other wall and squeezed the air out of my lungs. The sand molded itself, focused its force on every part of my body. I couldn't move, and I felt the cave-in trying to push me back against the wall.

The dust cleared. I looked up and saw the sand had slid away from under one of the slabs of concrete that formed the sidewalk. That slab hung over me looking for an excuse to slide down on my head. On the other side of the hole, framed in blue sky, was Frog.

"You O.K.?" Frog sounded cheerful, but he was twisting his cap in his fists. It was the first time I'd ever seen him take it off his head.

"I think so. Nothing broken, but it knocked the wind out of me. Hey, get me out of here, huh?" I tried to sound like it was no big deal, but it was. I was scared. I was trying to keep calm.

"Yeah, uh," Frog bent over to look at me. "There's only one way to do that."

"What do you mean?" I could see the tension in his eyes, and that made me more scared.

"Well, I'll have to jump down there, to dig you out. It could cave in again. And you think its hard to breathe now, wait 'til I land on you."

"Frog, let's go." My voice broke—"Do it."

He landed a couple feet from my face, the force of his jump pushing harder on my lungs. My eyes watered from the effort of drawing air in. Frog dug quickly, driving the shovel in with his foot. Me staring at the blade of the thing inches from my face.

He dug fast, but even so, the shovel only scraped my shirt twice. He dug down to my waist, and then climbed out and extended a hand down to me. By wiggling back and forth, I pulled one leg free, then the other. He boosted me to the top first, and I pulled him up.

"Hop in the truck." Frog tried to smile. I tried to keep my teeth from chattering. We got in the truck and just drove. After half an hour we stopped at "Big Boy's" for lunch. We talked about baseball, cars, food, jobs, trucks. We even talked about digging and accidents. But neither one of us brought up the cave-in. That could wait a couple of days.

Frog must have called in during lunch, because after lunch we went out to the airport job. Not that I cared where it was, long as it was somewhere above the ground.

The sparkling blue double-cab pickup pulled off the highway and onto the site. Unlike the rest of the trucks clustered near the sidewalk, this truck was free of all mud, all dust. When a truck that clean pulls onto a site, people take notice.

The driver's side door opened and a guy in a hardhat got out, but nobody paid much attention to him. He was just the driver, the chauffeur. The crew watched the passenger side door, waiting for the star. The door opened and the guy who got out was so short, he had to flip over on his belly and lower himself with his hands until his feet could reach the running boards. He looked like a skinny third-grader with facial hair. He bounced on his toes when he walked.

The crew hurried over to meet him, and the foreman, a sunburnt man with a white mustache named Gordy, brought the plans. The rest of the men, each standing at least six feet tall, with arms that made coffee cans look like toothpicks, all squatted with the foreman to be on the short man's level, and waited on his word. They were in simple awe. They had heard that this man got paid as much as a downtown lawyer just to crawl into a pipe a couple times a month, and they also knew that he had been flown in earlier that day from a job in Texas.

They ignored the man who'd driven the truck, a guy in a polo shirt, wearing a hardhat in clear obedience to the Occupational Safety and Health Administration (OSHA), the feared government organization that could, on the basis of violations found during a single spot check, shut an entire company down.

The man stood on the back of his pickup and introduced the shorter man. "Gentlemen, this here's Mr. John Carlton. He's one of two guys in the country who do this kind of work, and I guess I don't need to tell you how valuable his time is. He'll tell you what he needs to know. Answer him as quickly as you can. He don't have time to waste with . . ."

"Shut up, Lippert," said Carlton, "and go wait in the truck. I got work to do."

Lippert went back to the truck, clearly deflated. Gordy had been worried that he wouldn't explain things clearly enough, and the short guy would be some kind of a stuffed shirt that would listen, and then spit on the ground in disgust at how any foreman could be that ignorant, causing the men in the crew to lose all respect for Gordy. He was relieved to discover in Carlton just another working guy anxious to get the job done. Carlton rubbed his hands together.

"O.K. boys, what do we got here?"

Gordy unfurled the plans, and his men hurried to hold the corners down. They took their cue from him and all breathed a little easier knowing that Carlton was one of them. They thought about how they would have something to tell their wives and girlfriends when they got home, and they smiled.

"Should be pretty simple, Mr. Carlton," Gordy explained. "We're trying to run a new conduit under the road here." He pointed at a dotted line on the blueprint. "The old gas line is here, and a phone line runs here. Once we're done, they'll both run through the new conduit here, so they'll be a lot easier to get at. The problem is, we can't shut down the highway to do a proper job, and the soil won't hold a tunnel, so we dug a bit, then used a crane to push her the rest of the way through. Would have been nice if we could use a single piece of pipe, but that's too far to push. It'll bend."

Carlton nodded approvingly.

"So we had to come in from both sides. We ran one fifty-foot length of corrugated aluminum pipe in from the east . . . " and here Gordy pushed his dirty finger halfway through an imagined tunnel under the highway. "And another fifty-footer in from the west." He met his first finger with his second, all taking place under the imagined highway. "We got them lined up, and blew the dirt out of them with an air hose, but there's no way we can get in there to collar them together without working from inside the pipe."

"No problem," Carlton said. "You got the coupler?"

One of the men ran to a pickup truck and brought back an aluminum assembly with four bolts on it. The assembly was designed to fit inside the pipe. Carton would have to position it between the two sections, then, by turning the bolts, expand it outward so that it linked them together, the way a cardboard toilet paper roll can link two paper-towel rolls together.

Carlton took the assembly from him, and turned it over in his hands. "Piece of cake. Where's the hole?"

They went down the steep bank together, into the earth. The knot of men formed a protective ring around Carlton, ready to lend a hand should he need one, which he did not. At the bottom of the thirty-foot-deep ditch was a tiny pipe that plunged into the ground toward the highway. Its diameter, about that of a paint bucket, looked too small for a cat to crawl in, let alone a person.

Carlton rubbed his hands again and stretched. He took a flashlight from his pocket, put it in his mouth, and pushed the couple assembly an arm's length into the pipe. He wormed himself in after it, first both arms, one then the other, until his shoulders, torso, legs and feet disappeared.

Only after he was gone into the darkness did the men talk in hushed whispers.

"How much we paying him?" asked Jerry Parker who was scratching his head again.

"Be cheaper to buy the highway and close it ourselves." This from Charlie, the company man who was always trying to fit in by saying things he knew weren't true but that he calculated would impress the others.

"No way," said Gordy, and he scratched his belly. "Do you know what it costs to shut down a federal highway? This guy's a lot cheaper than that."

They heard scurrying in the pipe, and hushed up. Momentarily, Carlton's foot appeared. "Need a hammer."

Charlie ran and got one, and handed it to Gordy. He looked puzzled.

"What do you want me to do with it?"

Carlton laughed and the sound echoed out of the hole. "Put it in the pipe, next to my foot."

Gordy hunched down and set it there. Carlton twitched his leg and the hammer disappeared magically up his body. A few minutes later he came out, told the foreman the couple was secure, got in the truck and drove away.

The men went back to work, but held their shoulders a little higher that afternoon, the way men do when they've had a brush with true greatness.

There's this guy I used to work with named Sam who was about worthless. One time he came to work drunk and walked right into a backhoe. But even when he was sober he wasn't worth much.

I remember one time we were working at the airport, big old jets coming down not a hundred feet away. We were putting in another runway and we were running about a month behind schedule. Most of us could tell when Gordy was tense about stuff like that, and we'd try to give him some room and be sure to do whatever he said, right away.

Not Sam. Sam liked to walk smack into a problem. We were trying to put some drainage pipe under a ramp that the trucks were using to deliver cement to the crews working on the runway itself. Gordy got permission from the supervisor to close the ramp down for fifteen minutes so we could trench our way through the ramp, lay the pipe in, and back-fill.

Sam had the easy job. Tim ran the trencher, Frog and I put in the pipe. Don would back-fill. All Sam had to do was check to make sure the water would flow downhill.

That's where the trouble started. We were halfway across the ramp with an inspector breathing down our necks and Sam hollers out, "No slope on this pipe!"

Gordy knows we don't have time to go back and re-dig it, so he looks Sam in the eye and says, "Put the pipe in the ground and cover it up."

"But there's no fall to this pipe," Sam whines.

"Don't matter," Gordy says. "Put the pipe in the ground and cover it up."

"But water won't run uphill."

Gordy throws down his shovel and jumps into the hole with Sam. The rest of us tried to look like we were concentrating hard on whatever we were doing while at the same time edging a little bit closer to hear what was happening.

"Now look here, you pea-brained dirt-head, how much fall we got from the beginning of the line to this point?"

"About five feet."

"So that water'll be moving pretty fast, right?"

"Well, yeah."

"So when it gets to this screw-up and we ask it to climb up a couple of inches, what do you think it's going to do?"

"Well, I . . ."

"That's right, college-boy. It'll run straight uphill."

And the rest of the crew joined in on the chorus: "Put the pipe in the ground and cover it up."

When you walk into the big garage at six-thirty in the morning to get your assignment for the day, it's like walking into a Viking village. The high ceiling of the garage vaults up into the darkness, each steel support beam looking like a rib of an overturned Viking longboat. With no lights on yet, the power shovels, scrapers, road graders, dump trucks, giant bulldozers and front loaders, with their engines pulled out and tires off, and parts of their frames hidden by pallets of redi-mix cement or tools and equipment, look exactly like a grounded flotilla of Viking dragon ships. The light flickers from where Johnnie is welding on the far side of the garage and reminds you of a campfire.

You stand in a knot with the guys on your crew, bearded, powerful men who wear their camouflage overshirts and hold their shovels like ready spears. They crouch and talk in low, deep voices about incredible feats of strength: of the time the chain broke and they had to hold a cast-iron sewer pipe until the men could get out from under it; of the time a grader crew managed to get five miles of a gravel road graded flat during a rainstorm; of rescuing a man buried in a cave-in. They do not brag, they only recall what happened.

They speak of their dead, of warriors cut down by tree chippers, by buried electric and gas lines, by motorists speeding through a construction zone. They laugh sometimes and jab at each other with their fists. In the dark, some kind of violent northern light burns in their eyes.

At that moment, as you sit on your pallet of grass seed, you think that you would give anything to be a man such as this, a warrior who rides to battle on the wind, dispatches bureaucrats and meddlers with the swift steel of the sword, decides the course his life will take by sheer strength and cunning.

Then the boss walks in, flips a bank of switches, and the heroes you were watching stand revealed in the glaring light. They seem to shrink in size, and they cringe at the boss's words, fear the power he holds to fire them, to send them out onto the streets without a job.

The boss strides into the middle of the ring of men. With military precision, he divides them into their component crews and sends them off. "Heavy Equipment Crew One to the warehouse project on four mile. Heavy Equipment Two, back to wherever you were yesterday. Charlie, where's your pipe crew been?"

"Just finished up at the downtown water plant," Charlie says with a snivel.

"Head out to Thornapple then and help Ron out."

Charlie tips his baseball cap and shuffles away. The boss sends out the cleanup crew, grader crews, mechanics and truckers, and then, his work done, he adjusts his sweater and heads back to the office to wrestle with figures and papers and bids for the rest of the day.

As each man turns to leave the garage, he drags his feet, not wanting to leave the illusion and begin a boring day moving dirt. In the parking lot, they grab their lunches and swing up into monstrous trucks that growl their way out of the yard. The Viking ships sail out into rough seas, hoping things will clear up by coffee break.

We were digging a catch basin and the backhoe ripped through this high pressure gas main. The pipe itself was plastic, and only as thick as my leg, but it carried enough natural gas to supply a whole town.

When the backhoe ripped it, it started whistling, a high-pitched sustained screech that gave us an idea of how fast the gas was leaking out of that pipe. It came out in a focused jet, blowing sand around the hole.

Larry turned off the backhoe immediately. If that gas got inside the engine, it would have gone up in a giant flame, just like Denny's road grader did when he took out a main line in Allendale. Larry was probably thinking of the way Denny looked, how his body had melted together with parts of his machine, and how the funeral had been closed casket.

All this happened just off the service road of a summer camp. We had kids playing kickball within earshot. And on the other end of the field I could make out a guy burning leaves. Gordy sent Larry to call MichCon and have the gas shut off at the source. He told Frog and me to go grab some clamps and a block of wood from the back of the truck to see if we could close the leak.

We grabbed clamps, wood, plastic, hacksaws, anything we thought we would need, and ran back down into the hole. It was fun at first, like being a firefighter, risking our lives to save the summer camp. But after ten minutes of trying to clamp the line, and finding that the pressure was too strong for the clamps, we started to get a little nervous.

We crawled out of the hole and told Gordy it was no use, and maybe we ought to get everyone clear for a while.

Gordy was a company man. He married the sister of the owner of the company and he believed in giving his all, and more often his men's all, for the company. He scrunched up his wrinkled face when we told him that, and then, in a sarcastically pleasant voice, told us to get down in the hole and start building the manhole we were supposed to be working on.

Sure, we should have protested, but you don't cross your foreman unless you plan to quit soon. If he's teed at you, you draw all the worst jobs, so we set to work.

It takes about an hour to build a manhole. You have to mix the cement with water, unload the blocks, and mortar them together from the bottom up. The whole while, the gas kept hissing, blowing our hair around. Every now and then we would lift our heads and see if the leaf fire had gotten any closer. We worked very quickly, didn't talk, didn't screw around. We finished in fifteen minutes and got clear.

Gordy checked our work over and sent us back to redo the top two rows of blocks. Frog said "No way, man." Gordy got a five-pound sledge hammer from the back of the truck, raised it over his head and said, "Git in there."

We did as we were told, finished the job, picked up the tools, and left the site. The gas was still hissing.

HOW TO PREPARE A SAXOPHONE REED

Vincent J. Kunkemueller

You've been playing a saxophone *how* long? And you sound like *that*! I've heard grade school kids perform with a cleaner pitch, finer tone, and a far better sound than you. Let me see your sax. I pray, for your sake, that it's broken. No . . . none of the screws are loose. The pads and springs are in fine shape. Hold on . . . here's your problem, son: THE REED! You're playing on an *improperly prepared reed*.

It may look, to the untrained eye, like just another hunk of wood two inches long and half an inch wide, but to the true musician, the reed is the very essence of sound. It is the base from which spring the crisp notes of classical, the swinging riffs in jazz, or the down-home dirtiest blues that ever left the South Side of Chicago. Without the reed, you may as well be blowing into the hole at the end of a wiffle-ball bat.

To achieve the full-bodied saxophone sound that we want, ya first have to buy the reeds. That's right, you must face the fat, aged man with the goatee, who could not succeed as a professional performer and has been reduced to selling equipment to snotty-nosed kids who might one day actually *make* something of their lives. But fear him not. He is a broken old man who can do you no real harm.

Approach the counter and ask for a box of LaVoz number two Alto Saxophone Reeds. I've found LaVoz reeds to be finely sculpted from only the healthiest of the mighty *Arundo donax*. These giant lake- and river-shore plants are imported by LaVoz from South America to Paris, where great machines hack the bundles of reed roughly into the shape we desire: a two-inch-long, half-inch-wide piece of wood, flat on one side, with the other being a very gentle arc formed by the original outer shell of the plant. Thick at one end, but starting one inch into its length, a slow angle is cut that reaches to the end of the reed in a thin, delicate, fan-like shape.

Now you, like most students, will take this assembly-line product and throw it onto your mouthpiece expecting to sound professional. Christ, kid, why don't you just strap a popsicle stick to your horn?! The reed, right now, is only the block of stone torn from the earth, it is not Michelangelo's finished "David." A huge amount of fine tuning is still required. And for that you must have sandpaper.

STOP! Put down your Handy-Andy Hardware discount card. The reed doesn't need three hundred square feet of super industrial-strength rock-grit sandpaper. It demands the delicate touch of the finest grain *musician's* sandpaper, designed by woodwind engineers for woodwind instruments. This can only be purchased at your local music store, so prepare yourself to face the bitter old man behind the counter again. Ignore the dumfounded look of astonishment on his face when you ask for the sandpaper. You see, only the true artisans are knowledgeable in the uses of this fine-grained paper. And these artisans, cat, are as rare as a black man on a professional ice-hockey team.

Now that all the essential tools have been purchased, we may sit down to work. Gently, yet firmly, tear open the cardboard package. Rummage through the heaps of repeatedly folded packaging paper until you reach the bottom. Remove all the reeds from the box.

When the reeds are made in mass quantity, the machines will often goof and cut the wood wrong; or, since the reed is a living, natural thing, it is prone to the many deformities Mother Earth can throw its way. Thus, my little apprentice, we must examine each reed closely to determine if it is even worth working on.

Hold the first reed gently, yet firmly, between your thumb and index finger, at the base, or thick, end. "Thick," of course, is relative, since the thick end will only be about two millimeters at its thickest point. Hold the reed towards the light and peer through the wood. The center of the reed should have a dark, triangular shaped vein running from the base to the fan-shaped end. This is the heart of the reed, the backbone of your sound, and if it is flawed, if it is misshaped or it varies from its path in the center . . . ace it! It's no good. If you are actually able to wrestle any sound from this horrible mockery of a real reed, it will be deformed and ill-pleasing to the ear.

Once you have sorted through all of your reeds and kept only those with good hearts, you should soak them in a glass of water. You see, the reeds have had a long trip from South America to Paris and finally to your home. They are horribly thirsty, so let them drink 'til they are full. After about eight hours, when every fiber of the vegetable matter is bloated near to bursting, remove them from the glass.

(Here I must digress. Many so-called musicians prefer to soak their reeds in salt water. This, my friend, is sheer ignorance. Would a thirsty sailor drink straight out of the salt-infested ocean? Hell no! He would die of dehydration. So why soak your thirsty little reeds in a harmful salty mess?)

In your left hand, hold the water-soaked reed by the thick end with the fanned end facing up and the arced side facing you. Now, place the index finger of your right hand on the flat side and your thumb on the arced side. Gently pinch and caress the water from the pores by moving your right hand from the base (or thick end) to the fanned end, following the grain of the wood. The excess water should ooze from the pores, leaving the reed moist but not outlandishly wet.

Once again, hold the reed to the light. You can see that immediately surrounding the heart, the wood's "shadows" are rather dark, but as you move towards the immediate edges and the fanned end, the shadows lighten up until the wood is nearly translucent at the end. However, you will notice that these shadows do not descend from the blackness of the heart to the near translucence *evenly*. This is where your extra-fine music-store-bought sandpaper comes in.

Place the reed on a desk, table, or any flat surface. Make sure the flat side of the reed is against the desk, because if you sand anything off the flat side, you have *murdered* your reed. The intonation will never be correct and you will never score a gig. Thus, you will go hungry and die in some gutter outside of the Blackstone Theater's Jazz Showcase, your emaciated corpse clutching an improperly prepared reed to your feeble, sunken chest.

So, with the reed flat side down against the table, gently sand with the grain until the shadows are progressing evenly from dark to light. Of course, you must constantly check your reed by repeatedly holding it to the light. Sounds simple enough, eh? But there are still a couple of different precautions and rules about sanding I should mention:

Never sand against the grain. The chances are too great that you will take off too much wood, chip the edges, crack the fan, gore the heart, or somehow mutilate your reed.

Do not press too hard; you will remove too much wood. More reed can always be taken off, but none can ever be put back on.

Take a look at your reed one last time. Do the shadows progress evenly from the heart to the edges? No nicks, cracks, chips, or gouges? Great! You have finished your first reed. Put it on the mouthpiece and let's hear a little.

Ya see, professional music isn't all funny haircuts, goatees, and attitudes; you have to have knowledge. And with this skill, my friend, you now have a competitive edge, a secret weapon to put you on the top of the charts—or at least give you a chance to get on stage during Open Jam night without getting laughed off . . . maybe.

THE FOG

Robert C. Koehler

The river fog snuck up on Alfred Bower as he stood at the concession stand. Its cool, damp hands frisked him, sending a chill up his spine. Instinctively, he pulled his jacket shut, zipped it up, an act that seemed silly on what had been such a warm September day. Where had the warmth gone? Zipping the jacket just kept the fog inside him.

"Some coffee, please," he said to the skinny, sharp-angled kid in a T-shirt, leaning against the cotton candy machine, obviously unperturbed by the sudden chill in the late afternoon air. He turned his face toward Alfred's voice but continued lounging, so that Alfred had full view of the sweat-stained armpit, the curl of dark hair poking through the sleeve. He shot Alfred a bored smile, toothpick in mouth, as though to say: Go ahead and look at my armpit, old man . . .

Alfred suddenly felt nauseous and dizzy. As he waited for his coffee, fighting off the smell of cotton candy and rancid popcorn, he gripped the edge of the counter. A week ago, a similar wave of dizziness had sent him home from work two hours early. He took a sip of coffee and burned his tongue. The nausea passed.

"Dad, I'm gonna go on that Tilt-a-Whirl, O.K.?"

Alfred looked at ten-year-old Jake, a sapling in a Detroit Tigers cap, with a burst of feeling. Jake smiled hopefully. In that moment, Alfred understood everything about his son, with his soft cheeks, curious eyes, a head full of batting averages. He wanted to hug Jake. His insides lurched and he assumed the feeling was love.

"That'll give you a good shaking out," he said, returning the boy's self-conscious smile. Their eyes locked: this was their moment, father and son on their own in seedy little Riverside Park. It could only happen because the women—the mother and the sister, the wife and the daughter—were away on an Indian Princess weekend.

Then the boy ran off to the Tilt-a-Whirl, which suddenly electrified, lighting up the fog in gaudy yellow and orange and red. Alfred felt a piece of himself slip away. The chill pierced him again.

He turned back to the counter, hunching his shoulders and pondering the sharpness of his emotions. Organ music from the carousel, the other ride at the park, churned the air. Nearby, two men laughed at a joke. The kid behind the counter loaded the popcorn machine . . . *kritta-kritta-kritta* . . . Like pouring BBs into a skull, Alfred thought.

He gripped the paper coffee cup with his left hand, then realized he lacked the will to bring the cup to his lips. His arm was too weak.

What? he thought, feeling at first only a blank annoyance, as though he'd just turned the ignition key and gotten no response. His left hand encircled the coffee cup—he could see that this was so—but he couldn't divine the relationship hand or cup bore to his thirst. He stood for a long moment in the grip of a vast puzzle, pondering the blankness, pondering . . . the fog itself.

To the youth behind the counter, loading the popcorn, the customer could have been staring at a dead fly in the coffee.

Finally he tried to lift the cup to his mouth again. And again, nothing. *How have I done this in the past?* he wondered, absurdly. The fog around him seemed thicker now, wetter, heavier. Without warning, the weight of his fifty-six years tumbled down on him, out of the fog, setting off an acute inner howl. *I can't pick up my coffee cup!* Dreadful words . . . "stroke," "paralysis" . . . flitted across his thoughts. *Nooooooo!*

"I can't pick up my coffee cup," he said aloud, addressing no one. The words gave him a measure of control and enough courage to make a diagnosis: "The flu can do this. It can get into the muscles."

The teenager finished loading the popcorn and looked at Alfred. Their eyes met. "I think I've got the flu," Alfred said, wanting, incomprehensibly, that the pock-marked youth understand him. The youth stared blankly, without interest or courtesy. He had not heard Alfred clearly, had not in any case supposed that his job included making conversation with old, muttering men. An eerie stillness enveloped the moment, and Alfred imagined the youth's malevolence moving toward him like a miniature weather front: *You're washed up, old man. Look at my armpit, old man.*

Embarrassed, Alfred stared into his coffee. He thought about Jake, spinning around on the Tilt-a-Whirl, and felt nauseous and dizzy again. Today was their day, a father-son Saturday. *We've got a ball game to go to tonight,* he remembered, feeling his head spin. He slid his right arm across the counter, removed the coffee cup from the grip of the left hand, put the cup to his lips and drank the coffee. Then, as though he were scooping up change, poker winnings, he swept his left forearm off the table, pushing it to his chest and holding it there with his right arm.

He walked away from the concession stand cradling his heavy, useless wing. Surely the strength in it would come back. *Breathe deeply,* he said to himself.

The Tilt-a-Whirl relentlessly tossed his son and three or four other riders back and forth like some mechanical bully. *Why is that fun?* Alfred wondered, catching a glimpse of Jake's ashen face. The lights, yellow, orange, red, were smeared against the afternoon haze, adding a lurid urgency to his predicament.

The machine slowed down, stopped. Jake walked toward him, making a throw-up gesture with his finger, but beaming, happy. "What are we going to do next, Dad?"

Alfred smiled unsteadily and for a moment considered saying nothing to Jake at all. He felt heartsick at the idea of disturbing the flow of this day, of losing his son's enthusiasm. The organ music of the carousel churned in the air. A foghorn's piercing moan rose up from the river.

"I'm feeling a little punk," he finally said. A shyness now came over Alfred, a need to conceal from Jake his true condition. It was as urgent as had been the need, moments ago, to confide that condition to an indifferent, pimple-faced stranger. "Let's . . . uh, let's head back. We'll get ready for the game tonight."

As they walked to the car, he rubbed his left arm, trying to convince himself he had nothing more than the flu. He slid into the old Mercury, collected himself, laid the weak arm gently atop the steering wheel. Would he be able to drive? The task was suddenly so complicated. He proceeded deliberately, placing his right hand, his good hand, on the shift bar and pulling the gear indicator around the semicircle of letters on the dashboard: P, N, D1, D2, all the way to R. The indicator landed with a click, tongue-in-groove, and Alfred eased the car out of the parking space as Jake talked about his favorite player on the Detroit Tigers, definitely Jim Bunning this year, not Charlie Maxwell.

"Maybe Bunning's pitching tonight. Do you realize he could win twenty games this season?"

Dead stop. Left arm dead weight on the steering wheel, holding it in place. Alfred carefully bumped the shift bar back to D1. Forward motion achieved.

"I just wonder what's wrong with Harvey Kuenn."

"What?" Alfred asked sharply as he inched the car through the potholed parking lot. "What's wrong with Harvey Kuenn?"

Jake looked up at his father with a start, hardly expecting such urgent interest in his chatter. "Well, I mean, his average is way below .300 this year. Last Sunday it was at .277. That stinks. And Kaline's not doing so hot either."

In Jake's world, this was incomprehensible. He had no understanding of adult fallibility. He crossed his arms and frowned in distress, slumping back against the fuzzy gray upholstery and allowing himself to imagine the players in question, clad in glowing white, an inch or two tall as they appeared on TV. *Wham! Crack!* Balls flew out of the infield, skipped and danced along the outfield green. He rolled down the window and saw a procession of runners move around the bases, jab their spikes into home plate. The applause inside his head was loud and sweet.

"That game tonight's gonna be cool!"

His father made a sound that could have been a grunt; that's how Jake heard it, a quick low grunt of acknowledgment, grownup to kid. But to Alfred, the noise that came out was a horrible, knotted ball of sadness and frustration and panic, as though something monstrous beyond words was happening to him. He had driven the car to the mouth of the parking lot; when he turned his head to look for traffic on Outer Drive, he couldn't see anything at all. What he saw, or rather sensed, was the river fog, immediate and terrifying, as though it had escaped from his jacket and was now devouring everything to the left of him. The lack of feeling in his arm wasn't neutral; it was active and spreading. It was the fog itself, extending straight out from his body into the roadway.

In fact, Alfred Bower was having a right-brain stroke. Here were the simple, brutal mechanics of mortality: A piece of tissue had broken loose from a blood vessel wall, moved up the bloodstream, dammed an artery feeding life to the brain. In the scheme of things, it was the slightest of movements, less than a wave of the hand, a sweep of the elbow, but it added up to this: Going to the baseball game tonight was as likely as going to the moon. He wasn't even sure how he was going to get out of the parking lot.

"Hey Dad, did you ever realize that Al Kaline's name is on the New Era Potato Chip bag?"

A truck suddenly barreled out of the fog across Alfred's line of sight, and he jammed on the brakes of the rolling car. The fog momentarily lifted in a spurt of adrenaline and Alfred could see to his left again. He saw that Outer Drive was clear and pulled the Mercury into traffic, not daring to consider the wisdom of this move. His only thought was to get home.

"Dad, did you?"

"What?"

He had no room for his son at this moment. The latitude in his life had narrowed to a razor's breadth: Eyes on the road, hands on the wheel. *Don't think about sickness. Don't think about doctors . . .*

"Know about Al Kaline and the potato chip bag?"

Traffic light ahead. Alfred watched the deep yellow orb hang forever in the air. As he slowed the car, the yellow disappeared with a languid pop. He wondered if he was capable of judging distance accurately. The red eye of the traffic light struggled open. Red for danger. The car stopped. "No," he said distractedly.

"The bag says 'On the . . . ' what is that word? . . . *alkaline?* 'On the alkaline side'—on the Al Kaline side. Get it?"

Alfred didn't answer. He was immersed in the realization that there was no pain. For the first time since the attack began, back at the concession stand, he found himself wondering about this. No pain, just . . . *what?* Maybe pain would be better, he thought as he stared at the floating red eye, dangling in the sky in front of him. He turned his head to peer into the side mirror. The fog was back, like a rude, heavy hand in his face. Without pain, his condition seemed completely unreasonable. He was in thrall to an arbitrary force, which cut off half his world. "What the devil?" he shouted, letting all his frustration escape. He slammed his fist on the steering wheel and looked over at his startled son, who thought the outburst was in answer to his question.

"That's not a bad word, is it? *Alkaline . . .* I don't even know what it means."

The light shifted out of danger mode, red yielding sleepily to green. Alfred stared straight ahead. He thought: *If I unburden myself to Jake, no telling where it will stop. Saying it makes it real. Don't think about sickness. Don't think about doctors . . .*

With that same loner's pride that forbade him from asking directions, he vowed to see this trip to its end without assistance, as though that were the whole issue . . . getting home.

They drove in silence for several miles, Jake too hurt by his father's moodiness to notice the snail's pace at which they were traveling. He thought about baseball again . . . Jim Bunning, the lanky youngster on the mound, burning fast balls past the best hitters in the American League. He thought about how baseball players can be called youngsters even though they're twenty-one or twenty-two years old.

A car was double-parked up ahead. A huge, oafish DeSoto, devoid of life, sitting abandoned in the roadway, cutting off Alfred's lane and complicating his plan. He stopped behind it and looked instinctively to his left again: the forbidden direction. It wasn't that he couldn't see . . . it was simply that the universe ended at a line drawn roughly down the center of his forehead. Yet sounds, even smells, emerged from that missing, tied-off world. Suddenly a car shot out of it and entered Alfred's line of sight. Another came, and another. He didn't dare pull blindly around the DeSoto, across the broken white line and into the next lane.

Jake watched as his father, muttering to himself, breathing heavily, swung his body completely around, as though he were looking for something in the back seat. His father's impatience seemed to rise like steam as he performed this maneuver. Jake turned too and was puzzled to see there was nothing in the back seat except, wedged in the crease, his sister's Daisy Duck sunglasses. Muttering to himself, Alfred swung awkwardly back behind the wheel. Jake heard his father say, "Tell me when the traffic clears."

The boy looked. "Well, there's a truck kind of a long way off, not a big one but, you know, like a milk truck or something. And there's a car coming. Looks like a new one. A Buick. A woman's driving it."

"How close are they?"

"Well . . . . "

The Buick suddenly whizzed past them.

"How close is the truck?"

"Well, kind of close now. Closer than it was . . . "

Alfred drummed his fingers on the steering wheel. "Just tell me when I can pull out!"

"Well, you could've, but now you can't. Now you have to wait."

The truck finally rumbled past. "Now?"

"No . . . Now there's another car coming. A red one. How come you can't look?"

Alfred said nothing. The red car went by.

"O.K.," Jake finally said. "There's another car, but it's pretty far back . . . "

Alfred cranked the wheel with his right hand, gunned the engine and shot around the DeSoto. The effort seemed enormous, almost more than he could tolerate. He gripped the wheel hard in order to stop trembling. His mind felt like a Tilt-a-Whirl. *Don't think about sickness. Don't think about doctors . . . .* He repeated the words silently, thoughtlessly. They kept him focused for the last interminable mile up Outer Drive, kept him focused as his son informed him he had to go to the bathroom "kind of bad . . ."

"You could have gone at the park."

"I know."

"Well, we're almost home . . . "

At long last, their house—17708 Thayer Street—came into view. Alfred pulled into the driveway, hit the brake with finality. Jake leapt from the car and ran into the house through the unlocked side door. When his son was out of sight, Alfred slumped against the steering wheel, feeling every last drop of tension drain from him. The rest of the world was still moving, still heading up Outer Drive, but for Alfred the world had stopped utterly.

He sat for a long while in the car, feeling the cold fingers of his left hand tingle. The sensation took over the entire left side of his body, grew in intensity until he felt as though he were leaning against a pincushion. He had nothing left to do in the world but be aware of this sensation. It wasn't painful, just strange. He sat for a long while as though molded into the shape of a man driving, his left hand still resting on top of the steering wheel.

He started when, at long last, he noticed the hand. He was bewildered, disoriented, and wondered whose it was. *A hand . . . on my steering wheel?* He tried to slide out the passenger side of the car, away from that hand, but found himself stuck to the vinyl seat. Panic. Nausea. He leaned to his right, farther, farther, until he could grab the far door handle with his good hand. With his muscular, working man's wrist and forearm, he pulled himself to the passenger-side door. To his amazement, the hand on the steering wheel bounced along behind him, loosely, sloppily, catching for a moment on the Mercomatic shift bar, then disappearing from view. A voice inside him said wondrously: *That was your hand . . .*

Alfred sat perfectly still, huddled now against the passenger-side door. The pincushion sensation eased slightly, just enough so he could assess the moment. Is this how death comes, without warning or dignity, in the front seat of a '51 Mercury? He felt no pain, just deep despair, and so he sang. *Rock of ages, cleft for me . . .* Then louder: *Let me hide myself in Thee . . .* He sang to the instrument panel and the upholstery, to the door handle that he still clenched. He sang to keep from falling into the abyss, the missing left half of his universe.

Let the water and the blood
From Thy riven side which flowed
Be of sin the double cure
Cleanse me from its guilt and power . . . .

Then he eased the door handle down and felt the door, which his body rested against, begin to give. The next moment he was in a heap on the driveway, cursing and muttering. Goaded by his anger, he pulled himself up, using the car for support, and hopped to the door at the side of the house.

Jake heard his father call from downstairs.

The tone was strangely sharp, urgent, like when the toilet's stopped up. He went to investigate, cradling the baseball mitt he'd been oiling. He found his father slumped on the davenport, pale, his face drawn, his eyes looking old and deep in their sockets. He was patting his left shoulder with his right hand.

"I'm not feeling well enough for the ball game tonight," he said.

The words were crushing. Jake stood before his father in silence, waiting for him to explain what he really meant. This wasn't fair. Plans had been made. Vic Lassiter, his good friend, would be coming along. He opened his mouth, wanting to protest, but saw no give at the corners of Alfred's eyes, no room for coaxing or argument. He ground his knuckles into the mitt, luxuriating in the sad, sweet softness of the leather.

The boy's anticipation of the outing had been total. Most important, he'd seen himself there with Vic, not just watching the game with him but sharing his father with him. That was it, the ultimate thing about being a boy: My dad's gonna take us to the ball game, Vic.

Jake glowered into the dark center of his mitt, wanting to cry as he realized all this was lost. Only as the silence continued did he begin to consider the larger meaning of his father's words, that something was wrong. *What?* The boy wondered if he should ask but saw no room even for that question in Alfred Bower's pain-filled eyes. That meant it was serious . . . serious way beyond what a boy could know. The gap between them was unbearable.

Alfred sat on the davenport long after Jake had gone upstairs, sat there as the room darkened, staring into his soul, feeling the night commingle with his illness (he was still a day away from understanding that it was a stroke) and knowing that something vital—perhaps manhood itself—was being wrested from him. *Perhaps manhood itself. . .* He sat on the couch and felt panic gallop across the half of his body that still pulsed with life. He stared at his hands. Dull, square-nailed hands. Plumber's hands. These were the hands that had felt the icy cold of lead pipes in strangers' basements, snaked drains, wrenched open mutely defiant traps. These were hard, calloused hands, tempered by decades of pain and abuse, pinched between pipes, shot through with steel slivers, pounded, battered, blistered and broken. But for all that they were intelligent hands, wise with wrench and drill brace, jack and pry bar.

These were also the hands that had cupped a woman's breasts . . . one woman's only. These were the hands that had awakened him from a monk's bachelorhood, oh, so many years ago now, on a secluded piece of Belle Isle lawn, beneath a great, lonely oak tree. Staring at his hands this horrible night, Alfred Bower could remember that woman now, before she became his wife, when she blushed and sighed so easily next to him. He could remember nosing their lover's canoe onto the empty beach, stone and sand scraping against polished wood. He could remember the silence between them, charged with perfect understanding. Two pent-up people—a plumber and a schoolmarm, one with an eighth-grade education in a one-room country schoolhouse, the other with a Master's degree from the University of Michigan—wondering at this sudden, physical mystery between them, about to be pushed to the very edge of Christian modesty and decency. *You are my sunshine, my only sunshine . . .*

Two pent-up people, stepping out of their canoe. The man, at the back of the canoe, splashes heedlessly into six inches of water, feels the wetness penetrate his socks, hears his feet squeak on the tight sand. He takes the woman's hand, she rises delicately, the canoe rocks, she wobbles and lets herself fall toward him. *You make me happy when skies are gray.*

They lie under the secluded white oak, aching for each other in ways they never dreamed possible, feeling their embrace tighten and relax, tighten and relax.

The man strokes the woman's cheek and jaw and neck, first with the back of his fingers, but as her flesh gives beneath him, he turns his hand over—possibly apologizes for it, this hungry plumber's hand, more certain with a Stillson wrench than a schoolmarm's neck—and allows the softness of her flesh to soften and sensitize his fingertips. Two virgins, two Christians: They both know the name for this feeling now, wonder if they can stop it, know they must not stop it *yet*.

The name of the feeling is temptation. Surely it can be allowed to progress just a little further. Surely past the neck. Surely past the throat. The man feels the woman's warmth in the V of her throat, feels the breath rush from her lungs and form a sigh. She shifts under him. The man's fingers encounter the top button of her blouse, rest against it, then lightly, almost playfully, work it through the buttonhole. A sin, yes, but surely a small one. The woman shifts again, sighs again. Possibly she says his name. The sound she makes is deliriously soft. It envelops his whole body and he moans, a sad, questioning moan. Shall I go on? She digs her fingernails into his back, ten electrodes piercing his shirt, his skin, making his blood bubble. He undoes the second button of the blouse and the third and she does not stop him. Instead she sighs again, a deep sigh that's almost like the groan of a man at work, a man leveraging a stove or refrigerator out of the corner and onto a handtruck. Her sigh seems to leverage the two of them out from under the weight of propriety. After this, they cannot pretend they are strangers.

The man's fingers finish the job on her blouse, then gently push it back, over the curve of her shoulders, which undulate in light and shadow. A breeze sweeps in off the river at that moment and raises tiny goosebumps in places on the woman's skin that have never before felt breeze or sunlight. For a moment the man, ashamed of his crude, uneducated hands, dares not touch those places himself. But she says his name again and, like a child, he touches her. Each touch produces a fresh sigh and each sigh ups the ante, ignites his yearning. In delicious weakness he whispers "Forgive me" and cups his hands on her bargain-basement, working girl's brassiere. "Take it off," the schoolmarm says and his hands fumble around behind her, pulling, yanking at the two little hooks between her shoulder blades, which refuse to let go, as though stubbornly holding a woman's virtue in place.

The woman laughs, scootches herself up. "Let me, silly." And she reaches behind her back with deft, quick fingers and releases her own virtue as though it were the simplest thing. The brassiere, unsnapped, hangs loosely on her breasts and the man, finding permission in her eyes, tugs it lightly. It falls to her lap. Her small breasts, impertinent and free, become, for the moment, his, here beneath the stately and lonely old oak, rising up out of the grass in a secluded corner of the city of Detroit's island park on a sunny afternoon in 1941. *All this waiting . . .* he thinks. *All this time . . .* And then he can only moan "Oh God, oh God," as he caresses her breasts, buries himself in their soft and wondrous warmth. "I'm sorry. Forgive me. Oh God."

His hands. His hands. On this afternoon they went no further. That night, after he returned to his rooming house in Ann Arbor, reeling with excitement and shame, he wrote Rita Zimmerman a letter that began: "Remind me of it sometime, in case I forget, to give myself a good swift kick in the pants, when I love you too hard and too long." He was thinking about his hands when he wrote that letter, savage instruments of an uneducated man's desire. Rita forgave those hands, of course; indeed, far more than that, she worshipped them, understood they were infinitely more sensitive than any others she had known.

So Alfred Bower, the night of his stroke, sat for hours on the living room couch, staring at his hands in helpless panic, wondering what would be left of him when the retribution was over. Those hands, which could perform a man's work and a man's loving, sat limp on his lap, suddenly an old man's lap. One hand was devoid of feeling and both were devoid of will. He felt entombed as he sat in the darkness, aware of but unconnected to the world of honking horns and humming refrigerator motors. The loneliness wracked his body, sucked the breath from him.

He would have screamed out, but for fear of waking his son, asleep upstairs. Instead he cried, silently, uncontrollably. Everything he'd held back in fifty-six years of life seemed to break loose, burst past some control point and instantly liquify. Because he'd never once cried as an adult—had not cried since age thirteen, since the last switching administered by his father out behind the barn—the tears this night intensified his isolation. Some stranger, at once infinitely weak and infinitely powerful, was taking over his life.

When the crying finally stopped he went to bed. He moved clumsily, toppling forward when his good knee buckled at the weight it had to support. He crawled along the carpet to the bedroom which was on the first floor, only ten feet from the davenport. He leaned on his elbow against the bed and pushed himself up to sitting position, then, crooking his elbow on the mattress, slowly maneuvered his heavy body onto the bed. There he undressed (he must have, because when he awoke he was naked) and, after clawing back the sheets, slept the sleep of the dead.

The bright, late-morning sun stirred him back to life. He had no will to get up but sensed, dimly, a disturbance in the house: a clatter of pans in the kitchen, a chair scraping across the linoleum. Jake was up, doing something. The thought filled him with fresh panic and he swung his body out from between the sheets. His clothes were in a heap on the floor beside the bed. He sat at the edge of the bed, staring at the clothes, wondering how he had gotten them off.

Last night's episode was over. The terrible swift sword no longer moved inside him, inflicting damage; but he was left with a dull, half-body blankness, nothing he would have called paralysis, simply a blankness toward anything having to do with *over there,* all that was to the left of him. As he sat naked on the bed, he was aware of only being able to see out of half the window that was directly in front of him. He could see across the street to the Pieches' house, where a yellow sun hovered at the corner of a black chimney; but he could not see the branches of the blue spruce that grew in his own front yard. That half of the world seemed to be frozen over in translucent plastic, sealed off, unattainable unless he turned his head and placed the spruce tree into the right side of his vision, creating a new "over there" on the left.

He dressed with an invalid's awkwardness, jamming the unthinking half of his body, with no small effort, through sleeve and pant leg. He was forced to hop around the bed until he could support himself against the wall. Leaning against the bedroom door frame, he peered obliquely into the adjacent living room and saw his son . . . or a portion of his son . . . sitting on an easy chair, reading a comic book. He remembered that he had spoken to Jake the previous night, cancelling their ball game plans. He could tell that the boy, balled up on the chair, was still hurt by this. When Jake looked up, Alfred tried to smile, tried to mask everything with a look of love and humor. But the expression that formed on his lips was dry of those emotions, as though they were only shadows now.

Jake could not understand his father's look and coiled more tightly inside himself. When he'd gotten up that morning, he'd seen his father in rock-sound sleep, his face deathly pale, an arm flung off the bed. Only a husky breathing, breath dredged up from some far shore, gave evidence that he was alive. Jake dared not wake him and wished desperately that his mother were around, feeling her absence as keenly as a gouge across the heart. It was more than a matter of her knowing what to do. Her maternal presence filled the house, created the context in which men could relate.

His father moved strangely, ridiculously, leaning against the wall. At first Jake thought it was a joke . . . the bear scratching its back against a tree. This had been one of Alfred Bower's favorite child-pleasing stunts when he and Donna were younger—rubbing his back against the side of the house, a telephone pole, anything that was handy, and informing them as he rolled his eyes in mock ecstasy, "Well, this is what a bear would have to do in the woods!" But now the joke was a ghostly caricature of itself. There was no laughter in his father's face, just dead-sober deliberation. He slid around two walls of the hallway in the center of the house as Jake watched, then gripped the door frame leading into the kitchen and disappeared. Finally Jake sprang to his feet, clutching his rolled-up Uncle Scrooge comic book. His father, leaning against the stove, looked up at him and let out a low sigh. "I guess I'm feeling kind of bad. Having trouble moving around."

Jake this time understood his father's look—his eyes half-shut, his lips pulled tight but sagging at the corners. Pain and weariness were there, a hint of fear, but the greater part, stunningly, was embarrassment, as though to say: Sorry you had to see me like this. I'm suffering, but I don't want you to know it. Let it be.

So Jake, silently, and with a resentment deep and remote, agreed not to know that his father was suffering. He returned to the living room, balled himself up on the easy chair and stared at the bright panels of the comic book, shutting out the world with a ten-year-old's force of will. He read the comic over and over, letting the story squares fill up his mind, forcing all his sensibilities into them as though something were there to fathom, refusing to look up when his father clumsily entered the room and sank to the couch. His memory of this day, this turning point, the most serious and charged day of his entire childhood, would be blank. He would never know what role he had played in his father's desperate first moments of disability. But in truth he did what he was asked.

The man and the boy, broken off from each other, settled in to wait for their women.

Rita Lynn Bower entered the house as Laughing Waters, lugging a cardboard suitcase. Donna Bower—Sparkling Waters during this mother-daughter weekend of crafts and bunk beds and Indian lore—was right behind, pouting slightly, clutching her round pink overnight case. Both still wore their Indian Princess dresses, fringed, beaded, cut from brown flannel.

"We're home," Rita called, her cheery voice filling the room. The two males, in their separate corners—both in their own way thinking *We can see that!*—said nothing. Her presence, as usual, activated their identities, at once fulfilling and exasperating them. But on this day they kept all evidence of her impact to themselves.

"Well, you two bachelors, you. What kind of wild parties have you been having?"

Donna, who had argued with her mother that morning ("I hate pigtails! They don't look cute!") was the first to sense something was wrong. Standing behind her mother, fingering the fringe on her dress that transformed her into Sparkling Waters, looked from father to brother and knew they had somehow lost control of their time together. Her father's face, hollow, unshaven, ghostly pale, made her shudder. She looked quickly to Jake for understanding, but his eye sockets were also hollow, his features blank. He scowled at her in a way that said nothing and, saying nothing, tightened the dread that clutched at her throat. Her brother was Scowling Skull; her father was Secret Skull. For a moment she thought they must be teasing her. That's what men and boys do. But there was no explosion of laughter.

"Rita!"

Donna winced. The father's voice, jagged-edged and deep and desperate, slashed through this silence, slashed through the innocence of two females wearing Indian Princess dresses. The whole world shifted.

Rita Lynn Bower looked at her husband as she had not looked at him in fifteen years. His voice called to her as it had when they were strangers, before marriage and a family had settled between them, numbed the edges of their lives. She stood at the doorway, pierced, riveted to the spot, hearing in her name an echo of their marriage vows. This was the *for worse* part, whatever it might be, coming due. And so, looking at her mate, seeing at once that something had stopped working in him, she set down her suitcase and knelt alertly at his side. She took up his hand—the left one, which had no feeling at all—and squeezed. Her husband started to cry.

"Oh dear," she said. "Oh dear, Alfred. Oh dear."

"I'm doing poorly," he said. "I'm doing rotten. I can't . . . ."

His voice was soft now. The children couldn't hear, made no effort to hear. Donna looked once more at Jake, Scowling Skull, thinking perhaps that he was in trouble, or should be, for letting this happen. She had never seen her parents act other than as Mother and Father, two beings at either end of the table, he in his sphere, she in hers. It had not occurred to her that there was something more. She wished she could stop up her eyes and ears.

She heard her mother say: "I'm going to call Dr. Corcoran."

"No, don't," he said. "I don't . . . I can't . . . What would *he* do?"

Donna had heard her father speak against doctors before, declare adamantly that he didn't trust them. This time he wasn't going to win. His face crumpled in bleak submission. Then Rita was organizing everything, sending Jake this way, Donna that. Stationing herself in the hallway alcove—the center of the house—she telephoned the doctor, then the relatives. "He says he can't walk . . ."

Alfred, sunk into the davenport, felt his breath come in quick gulps. The children, who were about to lug the suitcases upstairs, paused at the stairway door and glanced furtively at their father, as though he were a stranger.

GRADUATION PARTY

Al Aviles, Jr.

Manny was more than glad to leave the stuffy party thrown by his family in honor of his graduation from high school, to go for a drive and a smoke with his pals.

"Come on," he said, waving a hand to his four friends to follow him, and they all swaggered out of the basement.

Outside, as Manny approached the pale tan and white Oldsmobile station wagon, he thought about how embarrassing it was to subject his friends to riding in the faggy, red, uncool family car. He was just about to suggest they take someone else's car, when Mike patted his big belly, hiccupped, and slurred out, "I get the back."

Ralphy sat in the passenger's seat, Ray and Rich—two pale white boys—took the back seat, and sleepy, woozy Mike laid out full length in the back of the wagon like a corpse, with his hands draped over his chest.

Manny started the car, and a deep-voiced, Spanish-speaking announcer boomed out of the car's speakers. Manny quickly switched the radio station from the Spanish station to a rock station, cranked the volume up, and started pulling away from the curb.

Ralphy leaned over and lowered the volume. He ran a finger over his wispy moustache and asked Manny, "Was that girl back at the party the cousin you were telling me about? The one with the kid? Man, she's hot lookin'. How old is she?"

Manny frowned. "Eighteen or nineteen." He didn't want to talk about his cousin, but he went on with a tired tone, "Yeah, every guy thinks Gloria's hot lookin'. That's why she's got one kid and another one on the way."

Rich and Ray leaned forward from the back seat. "That girl's pregnant?" one of them asked.

"Yeah," Manny said. "Two kids, *two* different fathers. She had to drop out of school. But she doesn't want to get married she says. Nooo. She says she's too young. Can you believe that? She's so stupid. But that's how the girls are over by the Back of the Yards. I'm always hearing about girls over there from the old neighborhood getting pregnant. Ya know, it makes sense they live near where the stockyards used to be. They're nothing but pigs."

"You used to live in the Back of the Yards?" Rich asked.

"Yeah, till I was six or seven."

"Why do they call it Back of the Yards?" Ray asked.

Rich knocked him in the head—"Because it used to be in the back of the stockyards, stupid."

Manny said, "Ya know what they should do over there, is that once a girl reaches thirteen, they should make her wear one of those chastity belts."

"Hey, man, if the girls are so hot over there, maybe we should take a ride over there one night," Ralph said to Manny. "I mean if they put out so easily and all."

Manny shook his head and made a face. "Naw, you don't want to mess around with those chicks. They're bad news and stupid like my cousin, Gloria. You'll wind up like my cousins Ernie and Louie. First, Ernie got two girls pregnant at the same time."

"At the same time?" Ralphy said. "Together?"

"You know what I mean, dickhead," Manny snapped. "He was kinda going out with two girls and wound up getting both pregnant. He lucked out, cause they both ended up getting abortions. And Ernie's only sixteen. From what I heard, his old man was ready to cut off Ernie's dick when he found out."

Ralphy squirmed in his seat.

"He works for the Park District, I think. He dropped out of school. Ernie isn't at the party, but Louie is. He's another dropout, too. He's the short, dark one in black with the little beer gut."

"They're all dark," Ray said.

"But this guy's *dark,* the darkest one in our family. He's our age. Last year he got some chick pregnant. She didn't marry him, but she still kept the baby. Last I heard, I think she moved. I don't blame her. And just two months ago Louie got another girl pregnant! What an asshole!" Manny banged the steering wheel with his palm. "I don't know if he's keeping the baby or if she's gonna marry him or what." He paused, shook his head, then groaned, "Those are the ones that give Mexicans a bad name."

"You mean besides you guys," Rich said, pointing at Manny and Ralphy.

"Ha ha," Manny scoffed.

The tan and white station wagon pulled into the gas station, two bags of ice were bought and dumped on each side of Mike's feet in the back. Mike smacked his lips and continued breathing heavily in deep sleep. All of the boys exited the Olds and hovered around the wagon's open back window with their thumbs crooked into their pockets. Manny leaned against the car's back door and lit a cigarette.

"Ya know, I don't even feel like going back to the party," he said. "What we should do is cruise around. Look, it's Saturday night, everyone's out." He pointed to the main street that was thick with traffic.

"Yeah," Ralphy said, fingering his flimsy moustache and bouncing up and down on the balls of his feet, "we should take a ride to the Back of the Yards."

"Will you forget about the Back of the Yards!" Manny said. He exhaled cigarette smoke, and the smoke seemed to hang around his head for awhile until it filtered away. Then suddenly, he thought of something. "Ya know what I should have done before we left? I should have swiped all of my graduation cards, taken out the money, and we all could have gone somewhere."

"Yeah, like where?" Ray asked.

Ralphy bounced on his feet again and sputtered out, "We could have gone down to Rush Street and gotten some hookers!"

Everyone turned to look at him curiously. Manny pointed the two fingers that held his cigarette at Ralphy.

"Ya know, you just better stay away from my girl cousins tonight. If I even see you *lookin'* at them, I'll rip your eyes out."

Manny took a last long drag from his cigarette, dropped it, and crushed it with his shoe. "Come on," he said wearily, and climbed into the car.

When Manny returned to his house and opened the back door, he and his buddies were instantly hit with the combination of the blaring Mexican music and the thick aroma of warm, spicy Mexican food that was nearly ready to be served. Manny hungrily inhaled, and the delicious aroma reached down, grabbed hold of his gut, yanked him into the house, and dragged him down the basement stairs. His four buddies followed, each sniffing the air, trying to distinguish the different smells.

At the bottom of the stairs, Manny handed the two bags of ice to his twin brothers and watched them race to the other end of the basement to deliver them to their father at the bar. His four friends eagerly followed the twins, thirsty for more of his father's piña coladas. He stood firmly fixed near the bottom step, hesitant to slip into the basement.

Manny's tiny Abuela (grandmother) Lourdes was in the laundry room, still tending to the food with the other women when she saw him poking through a bowl of potato chips. She wiped her hands on her apron and with rapid little steps charged up to the side of the unsuspecting Manny and began sniffing him up and down. She distinctly smelled the ashy scent of cigarette smoke on him. Before Manny could put a chip in his mouth, Abuela Lourdes sprung herself up on her tiptoes, reached up, and grabbed hold of Manny's ear. She pulled his scrunched-up face down to hers.

"Ooww!" Manny whimpered. He heard the cartilage in his ear crack as he bent forward. He saw Abuela Lourdes' stern little face jammed right up to his.

She sniffed violently around his head and with a clenched jaw rattled off in Spanish, "Didn't I tell you about that smoking? Didn't I?" She emphasized her words with quick tugs on his ear. "You're so stubborn. I smoked, and look at me now. I'm this little feather of a woman. All skin and bones! You think you'll always be so tall? I used to be taller than this, but those cigarettes cut me down. Cut me in half! You think you'll always be this young? Well you won't. You'll age just like me and your abuelo here." Abuela Lourdes nodded over to her husband, Umberto, who was picking through the same potato-chip bowl Manny had been picking through. "I won't be here to see it, but you'll age. You'll age like a . . ."

She went on, but Manny didn't listen. He managed to peer one eye over his abuela's little gray head, and he looked down to the other end of the basement to see if his buddies were watching this scene. No, they weren't. He could see them crowding around the bar accepting drinks from his father. Manny's abuela's brittle voice broke through as she released his mangled ear.

"Yes, go on. Go spend time with your friends before your lungs turn black, shrivel up, and die!" And she watched as her grandson walked down to the other end of the basement fingering his ear.

Abuela Lourdes turned to her husband and slapped a potato chip out of his hand. "We're almost ready to eat!" she scolded.

Abuelo Umberto was the second tallest member of the family (Manny being the first), and he had a full head of white hair that was neatly parted on the side. He wore round wire-rimmed spectacles that further sweetened his soft, fleshy face. He moved slowly, and he spoke slowly. Looking down at his small, feisty wife, he softly said in Spanish, "Let him be. This is his graduation party. Don't embarrass him in front of his friends. He's not a boy anymore. He's becoming a . . ."

The tiny woman cut him off. "Boys never grow up! Boys stay boys all their lives! It's the girls who grow up, grow old, become women. And the women do the aging for the boys, too. Boys grow, but they don't grow up. Look . . ." She pointed to the bar where Manny and his friends stood in a circle laughing and downing their piña coladas. "See that picture? They will stay that way for the rest of their lives. They'll never change. They'll never grow up. Ten years from now they'll be doing the same thing—standing around in a bar drinking. I think the boy's father is right. Manuel needs more responsibility. He doesn't know he has it so good here. He takes everything for granted. He needs a real job, not that part-time job he has as a janitor. What kind of job is that? He should get a haircut and a real job! If I were his parents, I would kick him out of the house when he reaches twenty-one, if he's not out by then. It's just for his own good."

Abuela Lourdes didn't care if her relatives standing nearby heard her. As was her custom, she spoke her mind anytime and anywhere.

"Let him enjoy his youth while he has the chance," Abuelo Umberto said. "He'll never be a young man again. Look at me, I've worked all my life and only now when I'm old can I do what I want. But now I'm too old to do . . ."

"Yes, yes," Abuela Lourdes said. "Nowadays young people have gotten lazy because they have no responsibilities. I'm not saying Manuel is lazy, it's just that the boy lacks motivation. They need to light a fire behind his butt. I thought he had more potential." And raising her voice up a notch, she directed her next sentence out to the relatives near enough to hear. "I just don't want to see the boy end up like some of my other grandchildren!"

The nearby relatives, who happened to include Manny's cousins—Louie, and pregnant Gloria—heard Abuela Lourdes, and they frowned and shook their heads, but no one dared to look her way.

Leaning toward her husband, she whispered sharply, "How can they face me after they have disgraced our family? Don't they have any respect?" Abuela Lourdes ended her commentary with: "It may be too late to change Manuel's ways, so they better start working on the twins."

At the moment, the twins, Martin and Mark, were picking through more bowls at the appetizer table. Their black hair was, surprisingly, still neatly slicked down, though their shirt tails were escaping out of their trousers.

Abuela Lourdes sweetly called out to them with outstretched arms. "Martin. Mark. Come here, my boys."

Martin and Mark looked at each other with wide eyes as if asking each other what they had done wrong, then slowly went up to their abuela, hands over their ears.

Abuela Lourdes scooped up a boy in each arm and hugged them to her bosom. "You're so precious, so innocent. We'll make sure you're brought up right. Do my boys love their abuela?"

Once again the twins turned to each other, and as was their curious habit, one answered in English, while the other answered in Spanish.

"Si."

"Yes."

"That's my boys," Abuela Lourdes said as she tucked their shirt tails back into their pants.

The rest of the party did not go well for Manny: the humidity from his mother's food dishes and the moist bodies crowding the basement loosened the tape that held up the CONGRATULATIONS banner, and it fell from the paneled wall in a crumpled heap; the monotonous, obnoxious, clamorous Mexican music drilled a headache into his temples; and the abundant meal had expanded every guest to almost twice their size so that now full, warm bodies bounced and nudged each other for space in the Riveras' basement, which was threatening to smother Manny. He excused himself from his friends and stepped out into the clear June air to steal a smoke behind the garage.

When Manny opened the gate that led out into the alley, he was startled to see a short, dark figure already standing in front of the garage door smoking. The figure jumped at the sound of the gate clacking.

"Shit, man!" Louie whispered loudly. "I thought you were Abuela."

The street lamp three garages away barely lit up Louie, who besides being the darkest member of Manny's family, was clothed all in black. Long bangs of hair rested on his eyebrows and partially hid the pack of pink pimples camped out on his forehead.

Manny swaggered up to Louie shaking out a cigarette from a pack and pondered if smoking here with Louie was worse than being stuck back in the congested basement.

"Don't worry," Manny said. "Your ears are safe for now. Mine wasn't so lucky." Manny gently fingered his sore ear.

"Oh yeah," Louie said. "Well, you're supposed to be the old lady's *favorite*."

"Well, I sure don't *feel* like it." He lit his cigarette, sucked in some smoke, and squinted at his cousin.

"Bullshit," Louie said. "You know you're the old lady's favorite." And Louie blew a stream of smoke up towards Manny, who was about three steps away from him.

Manny blew a tunnel of smoke right back down towards Louie. "It's news to me."

"Sure," Louie sneered. "That's why Abuela and Abuelo followed you out here to this neighborhood. Your family has always been their favorite."

"Maybe they just wanted to get out of the *Back of the Yards.*" Manny spat out the words "Back of the Yards."

"I know you think you're better than the rest of us." Louie threw his head in the direction of the house.

From the alley, both cousins could still hear the pulsing music escaping from the party. And they smelled the stench of rotten bananas from a nearby garbage can that cut through the tobacco taste of their cigarettes.

"Yeah, you moved to a better neighborhood. So what?" Louie whined. "And so what if you went to a better school? You're not any better than me." Louie's upper lip curled up to bare his stumpy teeth. "I heard what the old lady was saying about you downstairs. We're no different, man."

Through cigarette smoke, a hot and angry Manny stared hard at Louie. How dare his cousin compare them! He *was* better than Louie and the rest of his cousins.

With a wicked smile, Manny evenly said, "There *is* a difference between us, ya know. I don't go stickin' my dick into every dirty hole I see."

Manny got the reaction he had wanted. Louie's face darkened even more into a scowl. He flicked his cigarette at his cousin, and it hit Manny in the chest where it exploded in bright yellow sparks.

Manny dropped his cigarette, and in two long strides was upon Louie, grabbing fistfuls of his shirt and throwing him hard against the garage door. Louie's back hit the garage door with a bang, and Manny held him there, their faces inches apart. "You fuckin' spic!" Manny said.

Then it was Louie who grabbed hold of Manny's shirt in his fists, and the shorter boy managed to swing Manny around and bang his back into the garage door.

"Man, when did you become white?" Louie yelled, then pushed himself off Manny as if he did not want any part of him.

Stunned, Manny stood leaning back against the garage door, panting. He had no idea of what to say as he and his cousin glared at each other.

The back gate clicked again, and both boys turned and saw Abuela Lourdes charging up to them. She spotted the two cigarettes that were still lit at the boys' feet and crushed them with the heels of her shoes before corralling Louie's ear.

"I hope your children will have more sense than you, Louie! Hopefully, the child will take after the mother, which isn't saying much, seeing how she got herself into this mess anyway!" Abuela Lourdes threw Louie toward the gate by his ear. "And stop smoking! You'll never grow if you stay on those cigarettes!"

The tiny old woman then turned to Manny. "And you! Are you deaf or just plain stupid?" She reached up for his ear, but Manny had them both covered with his palms. Abuela Lourdes reached up as he ran past her and delivered a stinging whack on his head. "When someone throws a party for you, the least you can do is be there! Now both of you get inside, we're going to serve the cake."

Her verbal onslaught continued as she followed them back to the house.

"They're not old enough to wipe their own behinds, yet they think they can drink and smoke and father children. Youth! You can talk to them until your voice goes, but they never listen. Wait, just wait! They'll find out soon enough what I've been telling them makes sense and that I'm not a foolish old woman. You hear me, Louie and Manuel? I know what I'm talking about! I've been on this earth *four* times longer than you! You're still babes. Your mother's milk is still on your chins. Wipe it off and grow up!"

When Manny descended the basement stairs he saw pregnant Gloria's one-year-old baby boy dragging the CONGRATULATIONS banner that had fallen off the wall up and down the basement. The blue banner was bent, tattered, and slick with baby drool. Manny fought off a strong urge to punt the baby boy the length of the basement and instead searched for Louis, who had entered the house before him.

Louie was scrunched up in a corner at the far end of the basement, massaging his ear and glaring at the floor with his dark eyes. The moment Manny spotted him Louie lifted his dark eyes, and the two cousins stared at each other from across the basement. Each boy's stare conveyed the same message: to stay as far away from each other as possible.

WHEN THE FISH WENT AWAY

Susan Klaisner

Once upon a time there was a village settled at the ocean's shore. For many, many years the men of the village would leave their cottages upon the sun's awakening. And with their bellies filled with warm biscuits and fresh cream they would sail their boats out into the sea and their nets would fill with fish. The fishermen's smiles warmed with the air.

The villagers knew a good life. Fish filled the fishermen's boats, and their wives drove the wagons loaded with the bounty into the surrounding towns to sell the fish. Always their purses would be heavy with the coin of the merchants. And they would delight in buying a new hair ribbon or an extra bolt of fine cloth for a new dress.

Now the villagers had become used to their blessed ocean. And many of the fishermen had begun to miss their prayers. The wives too, had begun to grow fat with their lives, and had long since stopped being thankful for their blessings. Even the children were becoming spoiled with the shiny new toys they received, and their mouths were often crammed with sweets that they ate by the handful.

One Sunday the sun rose and found the church doors closed.

This was becoming the habit on Sundays. Why, even the pastor was sleeping in his bed, his face slack from too much wine from the night before. But this Sunday was to be different. For when the sun was high overhead the church bell began to ring, quite on its own. The fishermen looked up from their frothy mugs, and the wives exchanged wary glances with one another, their sewing idle in their laps. Even the children stopped running tag along the cliffs to look up towards the steeple of the church that had long since become gray with neglect.

Suddenly there was a terrible rumbling from deep within the earth, and the sky grew black with thick clouds. A great wind swirled the sky, lightning filled the village with an eerie white. That night the villagers shared nightmares they could not remember when the sun awoke them.

Morning found the skies vibrant and blue. The village was untouched by the storm, and the fishermen found the seas calm for their business. They set forth to fill their nets, their bellies full of warm food, and sweet-smelling pipes clenched between their teeth. But they returned earlier than usual and summoned all the people to the village square.

"What is it?" the villagers cried. For the fishermen were excited. In their midst was a strange woman they had found adrift in a small boat in the ocean. The woman was small and bent, with one of the men's slickers about her frail shoulders. Her hair was a blackened mass, filled with stinking strands of sea kelp. And when she raised her eyes to the crowd, it was plain to see that the woman was horribly disfigured. There was a great gasp, and even the men fell back from the woman. For surely when they had rescued her from the damaged boat she had been fair of face.

"Can you help?" she asked the people. "Can you house me here in your lovely village? Can you lay me in the warm sunshine 'til I am well?" Her eyes took in each and every person; later it was said that it was as if she could see into their very souls.

Now there was a great murmuring about the town square. And there was not a single eye that would meet the woman's. The men looked at their wives. And wives looked from one to another. And when the mayor's portly wife spoke, she spoke for all their hearts.

"You brought her here?" she screeched. Her pig-like eyes were on the fishermen's now-lowered heads. "Why should she live in *our* village?" The crowd murmured its agreement. Then she pointed a sausage-like finger to the woman and said, "This is our village, we have worked hard to maintain our decent God-fearing way of life. Why, look at you! You dare ask to live amongst us decent, genteel folk? Go away, you look a sight! Go away before you frighten our children or curse our unborn."

"A monster!" the crowd roared.

The fishermen shrugged their shoulders, and decided that the woman's face was quite ghastly and that their bellies were empty. So the poor woman was left alone in the square. The night came and sat next to her, and soon she found an alley to curl up in. And such became her life.

The woman never asked for a bit of food, nor an article of clothing. She just stayed in the alleys and the darkened corners of the village, forever in the shadows. And when the children would throw stones at her, she would not cry out. Instead, she would just look deep into their faces until they would grow bored and move on.

To the fishermen, the woman was nothing, and they quickly forgot the bent, twisted creature. For the fish were plentiful as usual and their pockets clinked of gold coins.

To the women she was an eyesore. They grew angry seeing her creep along the edges of the village. Often they would ask one another, "Why must she live here? Why must such a loathsome creature live in our handsome village?" Not one of the villagers thought to offer a helping hand, or a kind word, to the woman. Not one.

Then one day the fish went away. As quick as that. One morning the fishermen went out to their boats, and later they would say that they could hear the emptiness of the sea upon reaching the waves. Day after day they would take their boats out, hoping the fish would have returned in the night. But day after day they would return with their empty nets, their hearts heavy. Soon they did not go out anymore.

The women's ribbons became frayed and their once-fancy dresses needed mending. Worst of all, there were no more weekly trips into the nearby towns to sell their fish to the merchants. No more trinkets, no more gold.

The children's broken toys were not replaced. And their sullen little faces would fill their parents' eyes, and the children would complain, crying that it was all their parents' fault. The children had long since been spoiled of heart, and did not care about anyone else's suffering.

Then one day the twisted woman came before the people and said, "I can bring the fish back."

There was a great cry then, and the villagers jumped about the streets, their hats thrown into the sudden cool breeze.

"It will take three days."

The villagers were desperate to believe; they never thought to ask how, nor did they stop to think how kind the woman was to offer assistance after the way she had been treated. The people ran off in all directions, and a great celebration was planned. The woman stood in the square a long time, alone, her head cocked to the side as if waiting. But she was already forgotten. Night was approaching and she went to find an alley to sleep in.

The next morning the woman left the village with the sun's awakening. She sat on a rock at the highest cliff.

Down below, the village's winter food supply was hauled into the women's kitchens, and the men did the same with the stored ale. Many hours passed before the woman came back into the town. The air was filled with the delicious aroma of food, and laughter spilled out into the night. Again the woman stood in the town's square. Waiting. After many long minutes she went to an alley to find shelter.

The second morning she did the same as the day before. She sat atop the highest cliff and stared out into the sea.

"What exactly is she doing?" the villagers would ask.

"Why, she's looking for the fish," was the standard reply.

Then without thinking of how the woman was sitting in the cold ocean air without a wrap, they would cheer again, anxious to feel their pockets and purses swell with gold coin again.

That night when she came back into the town square, the villagers were setting up long tables for the celebration the following day. The third day. Again the woman stood in the square and waited. But not a word was spoken to her, not an offer of a warm bed, nor a sampling of the roasted meats. After a few moments the woman again went into an alley, the villagers' laughter and gay spirit following at her tattered heels.

The third day began the same. The woman woke at dawn and went to sit alone on the highest cliff. Musicians played their music as the villagers ate their fill and drank themselves into a stupor. The children threw all their toys away, for surely on the morrow they would have new ones! The villagers finished all their stored food and ale.

At dusk the square was lined with torches and the music still played. The woman entered the square and again she stood in its middle. The villagers' greasy faces stared at her, their eyes vacant except for their greed.

"Well?" the villagers asked.

But the woman did not reply. Instead she looked at them all. Waiting. The villagers looked stupidly from one to another, shrugged their shoulders, and continued to eat. Soon the woman left, but this time she did not go to an alley. She went back towards the sea.

The villagers congratulated themselves. Wasn't it grand of the fishermen to bring her in from the sea? And wasn't it kind of the mayor's wife to allow her to live in their midst? What a wonderful, God-fearing Christian town they had built.

Yes, they all agreed they had done a great service, and then the fishermen boasted of the fish they'd catch in their anxious nets the next day.

Then there was a great roaring on the ocean. And the villagers ran as fast as their drunken feet could carry them to the shore. And, then they saw her, the woman they had scorned, sitting atop a shining golden ship that floated just above the violently twisting ocean. Looking at the woman in a stray beam of moonlight, one could see how her face was indeed that of a fish, with black, bulbous eyes and shimmering green scales. Long trails of sea kelp became her hair, and the coral robes she wore billowed in the night air.

She did not speak a word. Instead she looked deep within the villagers' hearts and, with a sweep of her arms, the great golden ship turned away from the villagers. Then there was a great din of flapping and splashing of fish. The fish were of multi-colored scales, and it was as if fish from every sea had met here at their ocean's shore, for they were as a solid blanket of fish.

But suddenly the villagers could see that as the golden ship sailed away the fish and the ocean followed. The villagers cried out as dry land spread before them. But the creature did not turn to them. And the fish did not come back. And the ocean did not come back.

A heavy silence filled the air, and the musicians' instruments lay at their feet in the sand. The scent of the ocean was already a distant memory, and the villagers did not have to say a word.

ADAM'S DEATH

Keturah Shaw

This night, like every night since Adam's funeral, Irma had taken out her frozen TV dinner at seven o'clock and popped it into the oven. By 7:45 she had bathed and put on her cotton nightgown, slid two sleeping tablets between her lips, sat in her bedroom lit by the blue shadow of the TV set, and began eating. By 8:30 the sleeping tablets had taken their toll and she could float into the kitchen, kick open the lid to the trash with a toe, drop in the remains of supper, and then at last flee to the safe confines of her bed, wherein she would wallow in dreams till 6:59 A.M.

This night, as she drifted safely into slumber, wild images of blue still danced on the wall and tap, tap, tap, tap entered her consciousness. But she imagined it was a dream.

"Irma! Irrrrma!" Paul called from the side of her building in the dark, hands cupped over his mouth. He looked again around the sides of the brick buildings he stood between for a pebble to throw. Just below Irma's window was the distinct shine of gold. Paul picked it up, fondled the fine chain between his fingers, the tear-shaped pendant at the end of it.

But there was more there than Irma's precious chain: red lipstick, half gone, silver ring. And he thought, birthday present, 1970, and put it up to the moonlight for closer examination. Jade earring, just one. And he remembered: Christmas 1979. But his heart had begun a frantic race by now, visions of Irma lain out on the floor of her bedroom, bashed in the head by some stranger, and robbed.

Paul grabbed a handful of tiny rocks, and leaping from side to side, ballerina style, began throwing them one by one, "Irma! Irrrrrrma!" Behind him a light flashed on and a bald head emerged from the window.

"Some of us have worked all day, and enjoy some peace and quiet when we get home, so we can start all this shit over again tomorrow! Do you mind, fella?" the bald head boomed. Paul jerked around, distress spreading across his forehead. The window shut loudly, and Paul searched for more rocks. He found a second jade earring and closed his eyes.

Irma stood up, at last acknowledging her wakefulness, and peered out of the window to discover Paul.

"Paul? What the hell are you doin' down there? Come on in."

"I've been trying to call you all night!" he came in saying, and looked at the phone on the kitchen wall, picked it up, and smirked at the on-off switch, turned off. "Off," he said.

"Off. What did you want?"

"Got . . ." He paused.

"No, not worried?" her sleepy eyebrows rose and fell, her stomach felt tickled. She wondered if she were awake at all, standing here, in her unlit kitchen, looking at Paul with only the light of the television set that seeped through the open bedroom door. This could, after all, be just another dream.

Paul pulled his finds out of his pocket, jade, silver and gold, red, red lipstick. "Found these outside," and threw them on the table before him. "Why?" and he fingered them, touching the ages: wood watch, Valentine's Day 1984; gold pen, company picnic 1989; black rabbit's foot key chain, dinner while they were locked in her mother's basement for sixteen hours, 1989. Paul shook his head.

"I was throwing my life out of the window!" she laughed, since she was dreaming.

"That's sick. Irma, what's going on? You all right?"

"Oh, yeah."

"Then why you been throwing your life out of the window?" He touched the wood watch, Valentine's Day 1984.

"I figured it out. How not to live in sin. You have to be married. I want to be married, see. I want a diamond ring with a band to match. I want to be wedded, walk down the aisle. See? I need a comrade, a partner in crime," she laughed, hand to her forehead as she fell into a seat at the table. "You must understand, it's important that I marry. Can't live in sin much longer! No, no, no, no, no, and I repeat noooo! I must bond, so I can breathe easily in and out."

Paul dropped his hand to his side, and slumped in the seat facing Irma. This was crazy, wasn't it? he thought, breathing in deeply.

"I call myself dead. I've given up 'so far in my life' for 'so far in my death.'"

"What?"

"Lord! Why not be dead, since I cannot bubble in the beauty and bathe in the bountiful bliss booming from wedlock? Or simmer in the sumptuous serenity of spiritual splendor? Lie languorously and loose and lapse into lethargic love? Why not, why not, why not be dead? I want a ring. Not a ring-a-ling-a-ling ring, or a ring around my collar, or a ring-around-the-tub ring. Neeeeooow!" she shook her head, as it bobbed up and down on its own. "I want a shiny silver, gold, diamond, 'GODDAMN, ain't-that-a-big-ass-ring!' ring."

"When I am married, I will delight in the feel of this ring wedged into the brown lines of my finger, there for keeps. And in everything I do I will notice this diamond, silver, gold that has suddenly become a part of my finger. Like, I'll be washing the dishes, and through the sudsy bubbles, white and thick, I will see it shining on through." She stopped then and giggled, threw her hand to her mouth, "Oh, no! Not dishes!"

"Hey, Irma?" Paul walked over to her, pulled her wobbly head to rest against his stomach. It went without force, and stayed there motionless. "What's going on here? Is it about Adam?" he said, since what else could it be? This was not Irma at all.

"Adam? Oh, Adam," she mumbled, half asleep. "Oh, I killed Adam."

Paul closed his eyes, pressed her head tightly to him. "Of course you didn't." He was shocked to hear her shrill laugh.

"Poor, poor Paul. Of course I *did*! I lay here, this spot," she patted the floor with a foot, sending an echo through the house. "I watched and waited while he came out of me. It took a long, long time. But when he came out, I let him die. Choked," she mumbled, "poor thing, choked on my blood—*on his own mother's blood*. But," her head slid down him, supported only by his hands cradling it, "what else could I have done? The fact is, I'm a sinner now. And, really, all kidding aside, not even gettin' married will cure me now."

"Irma?" he called. But there was no response, and he guessed from her collapsed body that she'd fallen asleep. He raised the limp body in his arms and carried her through the blue light and to her bed. There Paul sat on the edge and watched her face, small and peaceful.

By morning he witnessed a series of outbursts. During each, Adam's name was mentioned softly, then through screams. Paul would sit closer to her, huddle her head in his lap and smooth the wrinkles from her forehead, rocking. He'd push the tangled wisps of hair from her face and just rock back and forth until it was over, since it was impossible to wake her.

As the sun rose, Paul caught himself drifting off into sleep, the back of his head supported by her Egyptian-style headboard. But Irma moaned, turned over beside him, and woke him.

At 6:59 A.M., her eyes popped open. One full minute before the alarm went off, as usual. Since she thought Paul's entrance through the back door in the kitchen had been a dream, it was certainly a surprise to see him sitting next to her in her bed, watching "Tom and Jerry" at 6:59 A.M.

She watched him for the minute it took for the alarm to go off. When he jumped, startled, and hit at the snooze button beside him, she said, "What are you doing in my bed?" though she wanted to say, "Do you still respect me? The sun has risen! What must the neighbors think?" and giggle. Hey, Irma thought, my sense of humor has returned. Does that mean anything significant? "How did you get in?"

"You let me in. Don't you remember?"

"No."

"Do you remember sitting in the kitchen, talking to me . . . in the dark?"

"No."

"Then you can't remember talking about wanting to be married."

"Fuck if I did."

"You did."

"No way."

"And Adam."

"Yeah?"

He laughed, "You said you killed Adam, then you went to sleep. I thought, wow, what a thing to say and go to sleep. You were really out of it. You're not taking drugs or anything are you? You'd tell me."

"Paul!"

"You were weird. I meant to say last night, chick, what the hell are you *on?* But you fell out like a light."

"Sleeping pills."

"You're kidding? No wonder. You don't really think you killed Adam, do you, hon?" He didn't look at her then. He hoped that was all it was, this sudden, drastic, even extravagant change in character since Adam's death. He wanted Irma back.

Irma stared at the television, shocked to know that she'd revealed that fatal secret, and wondered what else she'd said last night. But this was *Paul!* "I did."

Paul sighed, since at least this he could deal with, this guilt that made her think that the whole horrifying ordeal was her own fault. He could deal with something concrete. He could convince her in a matter of time. "Irma . . . ," he began the battle, but she interrupted:

"Fool! I killed Adam. I killed him, I killed him. My water broke in the kitchen, and I just stood there, my hands holding it all in. I panicked, Paul. I didn't know what to do! I meant to go to the hospital. I meant to call a cab. I had my bag all packed. But I stood there, wet! I was trying to decide whether or not to bring it home. I thought, if it's a girl, I'll bring her, but if it's a boy, he stays. Then I thought about its father, and his face. I saw his face, and I'll never forget. And if it looked like *him,* boy or girl . . . I stood there, wet in the kitchen!

"I had him on the floor, then I let him die. I didn't do a thing to help. Paul, I killed him, I killed Adam." Irma thought she'd cry now, but she didn't. She sat dry-eyed, next to a trembling Paul.

HIDING PLACES

Harlan Reece

A fine, cold mist of rain was falling outside, and a frosty haze hung over the mountains in the distance. The front of our barracks was not visible from the steps of the NCO club, but we could see the MPs leave with the dogs and reach their covered jeeps parked against the curb. From the steps of the NCO club we could look across the street and see into our room. The rooms on the first floor sat beneath a small incline, so from where we stood, we were looking downwards. I could see that the overhead lights in our room were on, but other than that, everything appeared to be normal.

We stood there with the rain knocking some of the starch out of our field jackets. The tiny drops of cold water caused me to shiver slightly when I felt them against my skin. As we stood watching, the last MP finally came out with a large German Shepherd on a leash. He gave a signal that they were ready to go and opened the door for the sniffing beast to leap into a waiting jeep. After the last jeep had pulled off, we headed back to the barracks.

Once we made it back to our room, Victor locked the door and grabbed the red silk pillow lying on top of his bed. He flipped the pillow over and unzipped the pocket on the back. No dope. A streak of panic swept over his face.

"Where is it—where's my shit?" he nervously questioned. We looked at each other in silent fear, and I began to imagine every awful possibility that I could think of. Surely they would find a way to implicate me also. I had to stop myself from visualizing being busted back down to a private. We were both specialists, which is equivalent to the rank of corporal—in other words, we were one stripe away from becoming sergeants.

"Maybe you just thought you put it there; stop bugging—maybe you put it somewhere else and forgot about it. Just cool out and think of another place it could be." But this did not help matters at all. It was as though he wasn't listening to a word I said.

"I always keep my stash in the same place—you know that," he emphasized. "We blew a joint with Johnson last night, remember? He was sitting on my pillow and I told him to raise his ass up, then I rolled the bag up and zipped it in the pillow. DAMN! . . . I know it's just a matter of time before they drop the bomb on me."

I didn't say anything, because now that he mentioned it, I remembered the sequence of events just as he had stated them.

He shook his head and said, "Besides you, Johnson is the only person that knows where I keep my stash—and stop pacing, man, you making me nervous."

"Don't get pissed at me," I said. "If they found your shit, both of our asses are in a sling."

There was a silent pause, then came a loud knock at the door that startled both of us. "Yo," I called out.

"It's Johnson, let me in man," said a muffled voice from the other side. I flipped the lock on the door and let him in.

"What's up, P's?" he shouted over the room.

Johnson was a tall, pie-faced boy from the sticks of South Carolina, very dark skinned, with thick lips and a wide gap between his front teeth.

Victor mumbled something under his breath, then fell backwards on his bunk.

"Damn, what's wrong with you, brother?" he asked while pulling off his gloves a finger at a time.

"I fucked up," Vic responded.

"So what else is new?" Johnson said, pulling off his jacket.

"They found my stash," Victor whined as he raised up from the bed.

Johnson's lips parted into a devious grin. "That's life, P," he said, bursting into laughter.

Victor's mouth turned down in anger. "That shit ain't funny, man, I'm in trouble —I could get demoted, plus a whole lot of other fucked-up shit." Still Johnson showed no sign of pity for him.

"Like I said, that's life, P. You got to learn how to roll with the punches. You fuck up, gotta pay the consequences."

Victor shot him the finger, and that seemed to make Johnson laugh even more. When he finally stopped laughing, he picked up one of the pillows from my bed and threw it at Vic.

"Get yo' pussy ass up, Vic," he teased. "Ain't nobody got yo' stash. I took it and you owe me big time."

A wave of relief washed through me. Vic leaped to his feet and tried to read Johnson's face, his eyes narrowing in skepticism.

"Don't be bullshittin', Johnson, O.K.? This is serious shit."

"Do I look like I'm bullshittin'?" Johnson replied with a straight face.

Victor held his palm out for Johnson to slap and their palms gave off a loud smack. "Thanks for looking out for me, J," Victor said on a more serious note. "Anything you want just ask."

Johnson looked up at the ceiling as if he was trying to think of something, then without cracking a smile said "O.K., I want to screw Felicia."

Victor's lips curled up in a boyish smirk, "Think of something else," he replied. "I'm sorry, blood, but you can't have no part of that. If I even thought she wanted to fuck you, I'd have to kick her ass."

Johnson looked over at me and said, "Now didn't you just hear this man say anything I wanted he would tighten me up?"

"Yeah Vic, you did say 'anything'," I commented. Victor put his hand on Johnson's shoulder and said, "When I told you that, I expected you to stay within the realm of possibility."

"Ain't that a bitch!" Johnson smiled. "I tell you boy, niggers and flies—the more I deal with niggers the more I like flies."

Johnson reached into the pocket of his fatigue shirt and pulled out a thin, rolled-up bag of marijuana. He gave the bag to Victor and told him to watch his ass. The rain had started to come down harder, and Johnson grabbed his jacket to leave.

"Hold on, J," Victor called, pulling a plastic medicine bottle from a desk drawer. He emptied half of the reefer into the container and gave it to Johnson. "These are some flaming buds," he boasted.

"I know," Johnson replied, "we smoked some last night—remember?"

I wasn't about to let him get out of the room without telling us how he pulled the whole thing off, so I asked him how he had known that the MP's were coming.

Johnson worked in the orderly room, so he had access to a lot of information. The orderly room had many functions: it was where we went to pick up our passes, took care of our administrative business, and received orders of our next duty station. Attached to the orderly room were the offices of our captain, first lieutenant, first sergeant, and in the extreme rear of the building was the weapons room. Johnson's desk sat near the door entrance that led to the narrow hallway offices of our immediate chain of command. The first sergeant's office was the closest, and when his door was open, Johnson could hear everything that was said. Earlier in the day, about lunch time, he had overheard Captain Williams and First Sergeant Gregory talking about a surprise search for drugs by the MPs. He could not find either of us, so before leaving the office for lunch, he removed the first sergeant's master key from a small box on the wall, entered our room, and took the incriminating evidence. He said that he hid the bag underneath some gravel in the rear of the barracks and returned to get it after the MPs had left.

After that day, we found another place to keep our stash; it was rather ingenious, in fact. Whenever we wanted to hide a bag or two, we unscrewed the frame around the light switch and stuffed our shit inside. It was too high up for the dogs to pick up the scent, plus the MPs would never think of looking there, and even if they did, they had no way of proving that it was ours. It was a perfect plan.

THE LAST POSITIVE

George Alan Baker

Terry has done a good job with the guest list: all of us at the same intelligence level so the conversation will be stimulating, and each of us with a fractionally different viewpoint on life so any discussion can remain dynamic without becoming volatile. Of course the wine is helping more than just a bit. There are only five of us, and we're up to our third bottle as the main course hits the table.

"But the issue is really where we draw the line between what is truly offensive and what is simply over-sensitivity on the part of the individual," Brian says loudly in his salesman's voice, like he's pitching another campaign for his agency.

"We draw the line where an individual becomes uncomfortable," Sandra insists; hers is a softer tone, whispers of reason.

"Uncomfortable?! On a daily basis I say upwards of ten things to the women in my office either as a joke or to get a rise, and all of them could make someone 'uncomfortable' when we all know there's not a snowball's chance in hell a situation would ever develop," Brian counters. We all chuckle at the point.

"But that's just you. If a STRAIGHT man were to say the same things to the same women it would be different," Sandra says and punctuates her point with a big gulp of wine.

Around everything there's glint and sparkle from the abundance of crystal: crystal candle-holders and wine goblets and serving dishes on the thick plane of bevelled glass that is the table top, and the tall sheets of glass that are the windows separating our warm little space from the night outside, and the gleaming pinnacles of the downtown buildings like giant crystal blocks pushing up into the night.

I reach for the wine. John watches the debating pair with a tight smile of amusement, and his deep chuckling comes out as a low undertone to Brian's and Sandra's discussion. Terry is speaking to me, low and close where his breath skims my ear, but it is impossible to separate what he's saying from the lively Brian/Sandra debate. There is also a muffled shriek and roll of winds from a jet coming in low over the city.

I force myself to swallow the last forkful of sauerkraut. Its sharp tang that was so pleasing at first has become repugnant and sinus-stinging through all the wine and smoke. A saxophone—very low and sonorous—hums from the speakers on the other side of the room. Sandra keeps glancing from Brian to me as if I'm going to jump in and rescue her, but my point of view is too closely aligned with Brian's to attempt interference. Besides, he's started using his fork to gesture with, too dangerous.

Terry has stopped talking and I flash him a quick smile as if I'd actually heard what he's said and was amused by it. Terry looks pleased; I delivered the right response and he was fooled, so I'm relieved. This becomes a pivotal detail in the memory of the evening—that I missed what Terry said. His eyes are so grave all the time and his face so hollow, and how he wheezes from the tuberculosis. His very pale skin, always oily, now with the rotten black/violet bruises that erupt without reason, seems like wax paste in the candlelight.

After the guests have all left and John stands in the kitchen running a sinkful of warm lemon water to soak the pans overnight and I'm clearing away the dessert plates from the table, there is the slightest twinge of consternation that I missed Terry's remark. And then and there without reason it occurs to me that I should have listened more closely because he is a positive. You should always pay every consideration to the positives.

The phone rings in the middle of the night and I waken immediately. For our kind, in this time, there is much bad news. It makes its circuit usually in midnight phone calls. So when my slumber is shattered I feel the awful thrill of anticipation.

John gets up and relieves me of the wicked burden of answering the phone. I am struck by the detail that John is wearing big wooly ski socks in addition to his usual paisley boxers. I don't remember him wearing socks to bed. Surely I would have noticed. How strange.

We arrive at the hospital. Sandra meets us at the emergency entrance. There is an icy rain falling lightly around us, and we stand under the metal and plastic canopy marked with the ambulance-park sign, in the blinding glare of outdoor fluorescents. Sandra is shaking all over—big, frame-rattling tremors of emotion that have nothing to do with the cold. She is almost incoherent, and it takes her a full three minutes to say three words.

"Terry is dead," she says.

The TB caused a strangling coughing fit which triggered a massive heart attack. His heart had been so weakened by his long bout with a rare heart virus that there was no hope—a rare heart virus unless you're an ARC* patient, rare unless you're a positive.

These phrases tumble through the chasms of my mind, knocking about for some sort of response. There is only a numbness.

From the hospital we drive directly to Terry's house. Sandra is not with us. John and I packed her off into the car with her husband and instructed her to call Brian. We drive in silence. There is work to do.

We start in the bedroom, Terry's bedroom that still smells like him, with all his stuff arranged in the patterns he wanted. John sets the cardboard box in the middle of the bed and we go to work. Into the box go the magazines from the bottom desk

* AIDS-Related Complex

drawer, a stack of glossy pages of photos of muscle-bound studs with aggressively hard cocks jutting toward other muscle studs bound in chains, flesh slick with oil and sweat. Into the box go the videotapes from the back of the closet, tapes with titles like "Powertool" and "Warrior Studs" and "The Size Counts." Into the box go the condoms and the flavored lubricants and the risque postcards from the dresser mirror. Into the box go the stacks of old love letters to Terry from past lovers.

We sweep all the rooms in the apartment, clearing away anything of an even remotely questionable nature. Neither of us says even a word. This ritual is an act of devotion planned carefully by every positive with his closest friends for that inevitable day. It is our labor of love for Terry. When his relatives arrive to set affairs in order they will find nothing shocking or disturbing or damaging to their memory of him. We cleanse him of his sins in the wee hours of the morning he died.

John tosses the box of stuff into the dumpster behind our building before we go in. I wait for him, shivering in the icy mist that gives everything a sickly pink/orange glow as it refracts the parking-lot lights. I can smell the decaying garbage, and there is a mental flash of Terry's pale, oily skin and how it felt so thin and rubbery when I would slide the needle into his thigh for some injection or other. He'd never been able to give himself the injections. John joins me, and as we climb the steps to the apartment he slips his hand into one of my back pockets, a gesture so warm and playful and intimate all at once that finally there is a rush of warmth in the glacial mass of my body.

Once inside I turn on the weather channel and stare without seeing. The pain begins in the pit of my stomach like a biting gnawing thing that expands and spreads and twists against my guts, and then every muscle in my body goes lax; I slump forward and the tears rush out. Terry is gone. He was the last person I knew who was a positive. There are other positives, of course; there will be many more. But Terry is the last one to die that I was ever close to. Like some Seventies science fiction movie, we watch the apocalypse advance, the negatives and the positives; the positives die, the negatives live on, coping with the horrors of the plague. It's all so unreal.

John comes back from the bathroom where he's been for a very long time. The sight of his face renews the rush of tears that had just begun to ebb. We hold each other until our arms ache from the strain and that sick feeling in our stomachs subsides.

Past the windows, the huge buildings of downtown are great gray blocks in the pink/orange haze of dawn.

SHEET METAL TRUCKIN'

Marion J. Reis

That sheet metal truck, Jim Bauer's sheet metal truck.

Jim got his license and the regular use of the sheet metal truck, always for going on long trips, like the one to the Ozarks. And for picnics no mode of transport was better. You could pile cases of beer, icing tubs, boxes of junk food, buns, frozen preformed burgers, hot dogs, condiments, utensils, and a passel of people—all in one vehicle.

We are camping at the Lake of the Ozarks. We are seventeen, and we have traveled there in Jim Bauer's truck—all males, our gang. We each have a case of beer, a bottle of whiskey, food for cooking out, and our camping gear. It is the middle of July, the weather beautiful—sunny, bright, warm—lovely. There are seven of us—Noel Schott, Rudy Novy, Wally Bauer, my cousin Jack Wuller, Wally's cousin Jim Bauer, Bob Philips, and I. We are not the magnificent seven, but we are rough, and we are ready, and we smoke, and we drink. And we are free to do as we please, to come, to go, to eat, to drink, to curse, to smoke, to talk dirty and sing, to worship whatever gods we choose! It's 1947, we are the class of 1948. We sing as we ride the green wooded hot lush hills of the Ozarks in Missouri:

Rye whisky, rye whisky
Rye whisky, I cry
If you don't give me rye whisky
I surely will die.
If the ocean was whisky
And I was a duck,
I'd dive to the bottom
And never come up.
If the ocean was whisky
And I was a duck,
I'd dive to the bottom
And get one sweet suck!

And on and on through verse after verse as we bob up and down the hills through the gently rolling country, in the back of the truck, we sing this song among others less chaste.

But here we are camped in a national forest on the Lake of the Ozarks. It has a longer shoreline than the whole coastline of the United States, Atlantic and Pacific, excluding Alaska and Hawaii, of course. We are ensconced at the campsite which we rent for an incredible buck and a half a night. We get to pick our own special spot off in the wilderness, high on a hill with the lake snaking around on three sides of us and a breathtaking view off in the distance across the lake. We're on a commanding tree-covered height far from other campers. We want to be alone, no adults for sure. And we are. We set up. Jim stretches a surplus navy hammock for his bed between two trees; the rest throw their gear on the ground. Some have tents, some have not. Most will just sleep under the stars looking up at them through the leafy branches of high trees lit by moonlight, and pray for no rain and good weather. Hot damn, it's a good time!

But night's a ways off. Wally and I strip naked and run down the hill to the shore. The others may drink and nap and play catch, but Wally and I like to swim. And what's the joy of freedom, if not the chance to skinny dip—to feel the current grab your balls and caress them in free float?

We halt at the wall of cattails which blocks us from the water. Wally arrives there first. So we pick our way, regretful now that we left our shoes back up at the campsite, barefooted, feeling the pricking stubs of the cattails as we painfully tread the mud-oozy shallows along the shore. We make our way, finally, to the water beyond the undergrowth in the soft caressing mud of the real bottom, and stand in awe at what we see.

There before us, the lake. We stand at the point of land, ankle deep in water, water on all three sides of us. To our right a twilight sky. Off in the distance, wherever we look across the lake at the hills which frame the opposite shoreline, no sign of human life, no houses, no roads nor signs of roads, no smoke curling upwards, no boats, no people—only the fresh virginal landscape of the wilderness. And the lake itself is an unbroken orangeish-reddish ochre golden, like the color of scotch whiskey, a surface mirroring the clouds and colors of the sky, just turning into early evening streaks of purple and lavender, blue and gray, orange and yellow with slashes here and there of crimson, ever so slight, tracings to excite the placid soul. Now and then we hear the close-up cry of red-winged blackbirds, and in the distance the call of a larger bird—goose, loon, heron, who knows, we city dwellers don't—echoes across the lake and rebounds again and again, but ever more faintly, from the surrounding hills. Oh, it's nice here! It's good for us to be here!

Here and there a small ripple of water or a ring expanding outward where a fish has surfaced to nibble on a water walker—whose tread is so light and delicate, the tensile strength of the water keeps him from sinking.

Wally and I are silent. We hear the guttural ribbeting of frogs in the cattails. These and the bird cries punctuate, only for emphasis, the immense silence that greets and enfolds us. Sweet and calming, lulling, Wally and I share the solemn, reverential moment. And neither says a word. And no one speaks except through being. We just *are*.

On that same trip we take a sideliner into a sleepy one-horse town of about two hundred inhabitants. It's a Monday morning about ten-thirty or eleven o'clock. We've been up, rising late, since nine or nine-thirty. After breakfast and a few beers at the campsite, we're in a mellow mood. We contemplate some mischief for the day. There it is on the map, Ulman, Missouri, in the heart of the Ozarks. As you drive through town, the chickens are right out there in the middle of the main drag. There aren't any curbs on either side of the paved road, just a patch of chat for you to pull up and park in front of houses, the one general store, a feed store, a tavern, a little church set back a bit more from the road. What a godforsaken little town! We don't even see people, just stray chickens on the loose and a sleeping dog or two, one just crossing the road now in front of us with its tail between its legs, head down like if it's been beat on a lot.

Well, we come into town creeping, slow driving, no sound, just as quiet as we can be. And we are ready. We are casing the place, on the lookout for maybe a cop on foot or in a car hiding behind a shed or whatever, hoping to spin out at a speeder violating the 15 mph limit through the block-and-a-half-long town. Look, there's a town pump right at the head of a small park and picnic area near a greasy spoon coffee shop, Vern's Café. Nothing here. Nothing in this town. No excitement. We look at each other significantly and point to our stash—no I'm not talking about marijuana. In those days we wouldn't think about that. There was nowhere to get it anyway. Ostensibly we're looking for ice—blocks of ice to chip into large chunks with a long thin steel pick and place in the open corrugated metal oval tub which holds our long-necked brown-glass bottles of Stag beer. Can't afford to be caught short of ice. I mean it's like the Fourth of July, man; and that's what our stash is all about. I mean it's not really the Fourth of July, but it's really just the same, like four days back on a Friday, and this is a Monday morning after a long holiday weekend just to make things more sleepy. We scan for a woman washing clothes—anywhere. No one. Nothing. The town is just dead, except for the aforementioned chickens and dogs. There's no ice house either. We're getting a tad bit pissed at this burg. About a half mile on the other side of town, we pull off to stop at a side road to reconnoiter on what to do next.

Noel Schott looks mean, recovering, red eyed, from a mind numbing, head thumping hangover. Subdued all morning, just coming out of it, he looks around shaking off his dullness. He snorts, gets a grin on his crooked face, giggles a bit under his breath. "Hey, guys, let's wake up the town!" But the rest of us are ahead of him. That's why we'd pointed to the stash.

So we turn the car around and head back through town, Hells Angels on a raid. We agree not to let loose until we get right in front of the tavern, just about midway into town. We want to rile the drunks especially, but watch the whole town come awake.

"O.K., ready?" We pull out some sticks of punk, light 'em, blow on 'em to keep the glow. Then we unwrap our stash, pulling off the paper with the Chinese writing and imprinted dragons—the red, blue, yellow tissue paper with the oriental labels gummed to the packages—pack after pack. We each have about a dozen packs. I mean big packs with about twenty or more in each. Not the skimpy five-count packs.

We're ready; we slowly drive into town, crowded around the corrugated tub in the center on the bed of the sheet metal truck. Philips and Novy are sitting on gear; Schott and Wally are standing, holding on to the upper rods of the truck, which usually hold metal gutters or down spouts or folded extension ladders, but not today, not on this trip. Jack and I are pacing, nervously squatting, kneeling. We can't stay still. We each gauge the free wide open space we'll need to throw the lit, sputtering packages out into the town, on the main street as we glide through, at the storefronts and houses and chickens and sleeping stray dogs at the town pump —even at the church, God save us! It's a two-hand operation to light a pack and throw it. So we tell Jim to drive slowly, so's those standing up can balance themselves.

Jim does better than that. He stops right in the middle of the street in front of the tavern. I mean where's the traffic? We look at each other and smile, a sly triumphant smile that says, "This is a piece of cake," with an inner chuckle over what we're about to unleash.

We light the wicks and throw together. Bang! Bang! BANG! WHOOMP! WHOOMP! Crackle pop, pop, pop, pop! A barrage of explosions, a sputtering chatter of bursting firecrackers. To the people of the sleepy town, it's Armageddon. Jim doesn't pull away, not just yet. He waits until the first dazed drunks emerge from the tavern, until the hens take off in fright, until the dogs fully aroused set up a barking howl. And screen doors slam and windows open, and kids come running and yelling from out of nowhere. We're laughing and guffawing at the turmoil we've created. Pointing to the bewildered folk who've come out to gawk at us in goose-faced amazement. They stare, hang jawed, impotent, as we continue to hurl hand-fuls of lit popping firecrackers at them.

Noel Schott is at his most obnoxious, foul-mouthed, abusive best. "Hey, you sons and daughters o' bitches! Wake up, you fuckin' hicks, you bastard hayseeds! Show some action!" He's laughing and giggling in that high-pitched tone of his. Meantime in our eagerness to see what's going on with the townsfolk and at the same time light more firecrackers, we bump around, stumble into one another, scramble for a better spot to throw from. Arms collide, and sure as hell a pack of lit crackers lies on the bottom of our truck at our feet. "Holy shit!" Philips screams, "Get rid of it! Get it outa *here*!" Fear seizes us all, as we crowd back and press into a corner near the cab and duck down behind the tub as far from the impending explosion as possible.

But then Jack Wuller, performing the heroics, jumps forward, grabs the burning pack, and in a flash pitches it over the back tailgate just as it shatters the air with a loud roar. Our eyes are blinded and our ears are ringing. Jim shouts from the cab, "What the hell's going on back there?" We're all pretty well frightened, no time for explanations. Jim just guns it, and we hurl out of town, falling all over one another from the sudden jerk forward in a tangle of arms, legs, and bodies—laughing and jabbering—relieved that none of us, at least, got hurt.

And so we hightailed it on the Ozark roads, bumping back to camp, recovering from our fear, feeling a giddy triumphant pride in bringing a sleepy town to life, just the seven of us, on a hot July day. A jumble of bodies, arms and legs in a sheet metal truck, a frozen moment of excitement, fear, and success—a moment of youth.

SARDO

Patricia McNair

It's all over this place, that "about to" thing. That thing that comes between two people who just met, or maybe knew each other for a very long time and only just realized it, or don't know each other at all. It's a look or an air or something. A glimmer. It's there all the time: on the morning train, a crowded elevator, a busy street. And in a nightclub like this, it's thick as smoke. You see it on the faces, in the poses. You smell it. Sweet. Heady. It's something you feel like a layer on your skin, a layer of something light and damp. A web that's moist.

I didn't notice it at first. How could I? The club is so big and dark. The only light really is the pinspot on the woman singing. The woman moaning. Doing her New Age thing: a cappella and without direction. Sliding up and down the scales, working her way to and between notes. If there are words here, I certainly can't recognize them. She, on the other hand, is very familiar. Marilyn Monroe. Bleached blond, wide eyed and hipped, dressed in black taffeta. It's a poor imitation, actually, but the crowd is digging it anyway.

They are rolling around in their chairs, only there's not any obvious rhythm, so they're all swooning and bobbing to something they've figured out on their own.

"It's how the yuppies trip." He's next to me, almost. Except he is on the other side of the wall. The wall separates the service bar from the club, and it's where I always stand. I like to lean against it and prop a foot up on it for an anchor. This way I'm almost closer to the servers than the servees. I prefer the servers. And Sardo, this particular server, is one of my favorites. I can feel his arm up the length of my own as he leans on the end of the divider, the two of us making a corner. He rests his temple on my head and whispers, "Now that drugs are out of fashion. They sit around in dark rooms with snatches of bright lights here and there, put on some eerie music that goes in circles and grates on your senses, close their eyes and go rubber. See? Tripping?"

"Wow, cool." I close my own eyes and try to go rubber—which is not entirely hard to do with Sardo standing so close to me, breathing and whispering and smelling and pressing—"It's not a thing like tripping!" I'm disappointed and I guess I spoke too loudly because a few people on bar stools in front of us swivel around to glare. Sardo laughs and holds a finger up to my lips to shush me and my knees give a little. I have to drop my foot from the wall to keep the rubber from taking over. I cross my arms over my chest and grip my sides, counting my ribs.

The lights are coming up now, a little at a time. Now I'm starting to see it everywhere. There's a man leaning an elbow on the main bar, rolling his glass in little circles while he speaks with Maria, who's laughing with him as she rings up her checks. Three guys stand in a triangle around a very small woman in clingy black bicycle shorts and spike heels, and she's moved into one of them, her wine-red hair just inches under the man's nose. There's another woman at the side bar watching one of the roadies pack up the sound gear. She's got both elbows on the bar behind her and she's shaking her long hair so that it swings over her shoulders and down her back. She puts one leg forward and digs her heel into the carpet, twisting her ankle and pointing her toes. The roadie drops an amp.

Everywhere around me, people are "about to." Not necessarily about to DO IT, per se, just "about to." "About to" as opposed to "already have." It's a beginning. An undeniable energy that you feel at the start of anything new, good or bad. Something that makes your stomach flutter, your hands dampen, your jaw tighten. Your shoulders lift and your ego soars. It's the best goddamned feeling in the world. It's the way I feel when Sardo takes my hand and kisses the palm and tells me he's so glad I'm there before he hops back behind the bar to finish his sidework and check out.

I'm still feeling it when the place finally clears out and the lights are all on and my friend Tosh has me re-add her checks. She's watching me through the smoke of her cigarette resting in the ashtray on the table between us.

"So," she says.

"So," I say ticking up the numbers on a bar napkin, "looks like a good night." I push the napkin over to her and point out the total.

"It sure does," she nods toward the bar where Sardo is marrying bottles and tossing out the empties. I swallow. Smile. Shrug.

"Yeah, well. We're still friends, you know. Just because I live with Warren doesn't mean I can't have friends." I'm talking fast, hoping she won't notice how my voice has gotten kind of high and tight, how my face is starting to burn.

"Easy, girl, easy. *I'm* your friend, remember? You don't need to explain anything to me. You don't have to tell me anything." She starts to gather up her things: her tip jar, her checks, her cigarettes. "You don't have to tell me a thing," she says again and leans over the table as she stands. She presses her cheek against mine and whispers, "Just all the details in the morning, that's all." She kisses me and is gone.

Kissing . . . kissing . . . kissing. How the hell did I get here? Oh God, his neck under my fingers. I'd forgotten about that neck—that smooth, sweet neck. Damn. Damn him. Damn me. Damn Warren and his hands in his pockets and his late nights. I dig my nails in and rake Sardo a good one. I feel the skin gather under them.

"MMMPHH." His hand tangled in my hair, he yanks. My head is loose in his grip, my body tightens. God damnit! I didn't want to come here to his studio, I didn't. Damnit even more, I did. I really, really did. My hand on his chest now, I push against him. He tugs my hair again yet pulls me in, wraps himself around me. If anyone were watching, they'd hardly notice the struggle, it's so small, so short. He's sturdy. Feet wide. Shoulders squared. He's got me now. Inside of him. I'm a seam running up his center and he folds around me. My toes barely touch the floor and I'm little compared to him. So little. Tucked away in the envelope of him.

"Sardo." That name, sometime I'll ask him about it. Now I pull back my head and look at him. He swims. Cloudy. Milky. He unwinds his hand from my hair and touches the gouge I've made in his neck.

"Tsssssss," he hisses through his teeth. I touch it too, and it's cool, the blood, but his neck is hot. All the while he is holding me with one arm. I barely need to support myself. I don't want to. Too much effort. Too much control. Too much knowledge of where I am, who I am and who he is not. He lifts me. My legs no longer need strength. They dangle over his arm. Dangling like my will power, my discipline, my flagging sense of commitment.

This isn't why I was here—it isn't! He moves quickly with me in his arms. He doesn't walk fast, he steps wide. His sculptures blur by me: wire, latex. I haven't even looked at them. He said he'd been working on something new, wouldn't I like to see? Trying new things. I felt a bubble in my chest. I was an old thing.

"Ah, you smile." His eyes are on my face. He kneels on the floor and arranges me on the drop cloth. Spreads me out like a gown he'd been carrying over his arms, one he's trying not to crease. I let him. It's better this way. If I make no effort, my guilt diminishes. Like when the neighbor's cat follows you home—inside your apartment—it's not your fault he's there. And if you leave the door open and he still refuses to leave, well, at least you've tried.

So it's like my door was open and Sardo decided to stay.

"It was my grandmother's maiden name. My family is big on that kind of honor. Tradition." We were still on the floor, there was only the light from the city outside the undraped window. It was three, maybe four in the morning. He pulled the drop cloth over our legs. I wanted to tell him that it was the name of an oil my mother used to pour in her bath and that something about him reminded me of it. Spicy, aromatic, smooth. Exotic. But perhaps he knew that already. Maybe as kids, even in the small Greek village he was from, his friends would tease him. Call him Bubbles or Softy or something.

Instead I said, "That's nice. I wish my name was something like that. Had some sentiment attached to it, some special story to go with each new introduction." I meant it. I never considered before that maybe why my name was wrong was because it had no history, no grounding. It was way too airy.

"But it's a very pretty name. Creessteena." There it was. The subtle stretch. Sardo's accent was nearly gone, he'd lived here twenty-five years, but he knew enough about when to still use it.

"Yeah, I guess it's O.K." One thing I learned about Sardo the last time—two years ago when we were steady lovers, more or less—was never to sound insecure. He admired strength. One wavery "well-ll" was as good as a cold shower to this man. "No, I mean, I really do like it. It's just that it doesn't *come* from anywhere."

"Creessteena. You will have to give it it's life. From here on, people will be named for you. How's that, little flower?"

"That's nice." I was talking about "little flower," he was talking about his prophecy. He pushed up on his elbow and reached around to the stereo under the window. Guitars played. Flamenco or gypsy or something else as beautiful and sad and full. When he settled back down, I rested my face on his chest. I felt his breath in my hair. "So what's new, Sardo? How have you been?"

"Lonely. Hungry."

I laughed. This was not a man to go lonely. At least, not alone.

"No, I mean it. It's been a long time since I've been content with anyone. With anything. Not since—"

"All right, hold it." I sat up and tucked the drop cloth under my arms, across my chest. "Now don't go telling me that since we broke up—shit, not even broke up, we weren't even *going* together—that you have been so 'lonely'." I swooned with the word, played it up.

"O.K., little flower. O.K." He pulled me back down next to him and cradled my head on his shoulder. "Not really ever since," he stroked my face. I love it when they touch my face. "But when I saw you tonight . . . Yes, it's true that not always was I thinking about you. When I don't see, I don't want. But tonight, when I saw . . . *I wanted.* And that's what has been missing. Not you. Just wanting you."

Missing the want. Something flashed inside me. That's exactly what it was.

"And you? You've been living with someone now, yes?" He crooked his finger under my chin and tried to get me to look at him. I didn't.

"Yes."

"It's going well?" This time I didn't laugh. To Sardo the question was not a silly one. To him, a person could be happy in love and still given to desires. A strong person. I wasn't that strong.

"It's fine."

"Good," he said, choosing to ignore my hesitancy. It's easier for him that way. Less messy. "Then as long as he treats you well. He does treat you well, doesn't he? Of course he does, or you would leave. As long as he treats you well, I'm happy for you. If he doesn't, you come to me."

That's just what I did, Sardo, dear. But of course I didn't tell him that.

"Now, come. See my work." He stood up and crossed the room. I watched the backs of his legs, his ass. His broad shoulders. Here was a person who looked good naked. I put on his T-shirt before following him.

"What do you call this?" It was an old typewriter, black and manual, with a microphone attached somehow to the carriage. The spongy part of the mike, the part you speak into, was caught in an extra large mousetrap. The mousetrap was painted red, white and blue.

"That's called 'News at Eleven.' Inspired by the Persian Gulf Crisis." He smiled. I laughed. He wasn't easily offended when it came to his art. He figured if people laughed, at least they were paying some kind of attention, giving it some thought. And at the very least, they were entertained. "Good, you like it."

"Yes," I said. We moved over to a grocery cart. I think I noticed it when we first came in, out of the corner of my eye. I thought it was for legitimate use. Now

I could see in the dim light from the windows that it was more than a cart. "Turn on a light," I whispered, like the sculpture was sleeping or something. He reached under the cart's handle and flicked a switch. In the little compartment where one seats her children, or her purse, was one of those "bar open" lights. The one that's a miniature street light with a sad-faced clown who is really supposed to be a wino, probably, leaning against it and frowning through his painted smile. His nose glowed red from the bulb inside. At the base of the cart, a girdle was stretched around the bottom of the basket. It was huge!

"Where—" I pointed and looked at the artist.

"Don't ask. It's not a very pretty story." He rubbed his hands together and put them on his hips.

Inside the cart was a Tony Home-Permanent kit, a package of children's underwear with cartoon animals on them, a man's pair of boxer shorts dotted with tiny Chicago Bears emblems, a box of macaroni and cheese, and a three-inch square of simulated wood paneling with the same size patch of shag carpeting glued to its back. And above it all, suspended from the ceiling with fish-line or something was a bag made out of bubble wrap. It was cloudy. Transparent yet white. In the bag was the wildest get-up I'd ever seen. It was skimpy and red and feathered, holes in the most revealing places; the center of each cup of the bra, two high-cut holes for the legs, one in between, netting stretched between the top and the bottom. Even through the plastic, though, I could tell it was not cheap. It shone like silk— it probably was—and for at least that reason, it did not look sleazy. It had a certain elegance in its overstatement.

"Wow." It was more like a breath than a word.

"Exactly the response I was hoping for." He clapped, rocked back on his bare heels. "I call it 'Split-level Fantasy'. Or, in case the audience is somewhat dim— 'Suburban Dream'. I think it's my favorite."

"Wow," I said again. Sardo moved around me and began adjusting things. He turned off the light, propped the carpeted panel up straighter in the basket, checked the fishing line. I heard him hum. He hummed when he was happy, when he concentrated, when he was intense. He hummed when he made love. Funny, I just then thought of that. Could it be that I never noticed it before? The sound of Sardo humming in my ear gave way to other sounds. Warren sounds. Grunts. No words. No names. A kind of held-back sound. Like just before a sneeze. Or a fall.

"I better get going now." I kissed Sardo on the shoulder as he leaned over his work. He patted his hand on the same spot. I dressed quietly and let myself out.

LOVIE OF LILAC FARM

Don Gennaro De Grazia

"The woods are full of wardens."
—Jack Kerouac
Lonesome Traveler

In the TV cartoons it's a mastiff's doghouse that the cat always lands in after his anti-mouse catapult backfires. Whenever things seem like they can't get any worse for a cartoon cat, there's always a big, tan mastiff waiting around the corner.

And that's kind of the way Lovie was. She'd scare the shit out of any stranger that showed up on our property with her big jowely jaws. As big as she was, with all her muscles rippling underneath her short-coated skin, and all her nipples hanging down below, she looked sort of like a cow, a killer cow. And when she scared people she wasn't just playing, she was ready to eat them if they didn't stop. But with me and my family—let me just tell you. I remember how she used to let my little sister ride her around like a horse through our yard. The yard was never mowed. That's when my sister was just a baby and things were probably as close as they ever got to being the way my dad had wanted them to be.

You see, he made a stack of cash back when he owned all-night diners on the Chicago Westside. Then he decided to sell them all and move us out to the country —way up north in Harding County, right next to Wisconsin. That's when I was a kid, and my mom was pregnant with my sister. The place we moved into was an old farmhouse in the middle of forty acres of thick woods and meadows. There was a big red barn and a long, white-roofed stable in the same clearing as the house. My dad bought a couple of Shetland ponies, and some sheep, and a goose, and a goat, and a whole bunch of dogs for us to play with. The idea was that he wouldn't work—him and my mom would just spend their time raising me and the baby, and he'd paint. Pictures. I'm not kidding, he painted—nature stuff. It didn't look real, but, you know, it wasn't supposed to. So, in that respect, it was good.

But he didn't end up painting much. I mean, that place was crazy. One time Lovie, the killer cow, jumped into this tall pen made out of chicken wire and two-by-fours that my dad had built in the barn for the sheep to stay in during the winter. It was the middle of a gray cold day and me and my dad were in the house, sitting by the fireplace playing Monopoly when we heard all this commotion. All our dogs were barking, and man, we had a lot of dogs—mutts of every shape and size: smooth-skinned, long-haired, pointy-eared, floppy-eared, fluffy black-and-white sheepdogs, spikey-coated shepherds, and one huge, dumb, long-legged Irish wolf-hound with scruffy salt-and-pepper hair.

After me and my dad threw our coats on we tore outside to see what the hell was going on. There was so much snow on the ground that it took both of us to pull the barn door open and my hands stuck to the metal handle. When we got inside and my dad yanked down on the lightbulb string, we could see that all our dogs were standing up on their hind legs, leaning on their front paws against the wire and the boards of the sheep pen. They were all barking at once—yip, yap, rolf, woof, bow-wow-wow. You could see their breath puffing through the silver wire, and they didn't even act like they knew we were there.

Like I said, Lovie had gotten into the pen. When we pushed past the dogs and looked in, we could see that all the sheep were huddled into the corner closest to us, except for one. That one was standing in the far corner while Lovie ate its leg. I mean, they were both just standing there, calmly it looked like, while Lovie chewed and ate off of the sheep's bloody hind leg the same way you would eat a turkey drumstick.

As soon as Lovie saw us, though, she stopped, and got this (man, it's the only way I can put it) sheepish look on her face, like some fat little kid with her hand stuck in the cookie jar. My dad unlatched the door to the pen and started yelling at Lovie "Bad dog!" and she just crouched down as low as she could get and slinked out of there, giving us those dog eyes, and licking her bloody chops.

Well, that sheep was fucked. I mean, there wasn't anything left on that leg but tendons and bones. So my dad went into the house and got the shotgun. I think he was actually a little bit happy to finally get the chance to use it. He'd bought it out of the want ads when we first moved there. Seemed like you should have a gun if you lived on a farm. But it turned out to be some sort of weird, undersized gun, and the shells the guy at the sporting store sold him were too powerful. So when he came back out and shot the sheep, the gun jumped back and knocked him on his ass. The metal around the sights cut deep into the skin between the thumb and forefinger of his left hand, so we had to rush him to the hospital to get stitched up.

He was all pissed off, too, not just because of his hand, but because he'd lost the sheep. That was one less thing he had, I guess. So, after they let him out of the emergency room with his hand all bundled up in white bandages, he made my mom drive us way the fuck out to Kincaid County where there was this little store that sold butcher tools. He looked around at all the evil blades hanging off the pegboard walls and selected a few. He even bought a few books on the subject. But he didn't know what the hell he was doing.

When we got home he dragged the sheep carcass back behind the house and started butchering it. He made me stand out there and read to him from one of the books he'd bought too. But the whole thing just turned into such a bloody mess that we ended up whistling for the dogs to come and eat the thing, which they were happy to do.

First time I ever saw my sister, Stacy, was in the car, when me and my dad brought her and my mom home from the hospital. As we drove, her head fell to one side and she looked up with blank, bright blue eyes that shocked me, like some absolutely real thing that had somehow snuck its way into a dream. They were my dad's eyes, and it just gave me the creeps, I guess, to see a grown man's eyeballs looking out from a bald little baby girl's head.

When we brought her home Lovie wanted to eat her—she was barking and drooling and baring her big yellow fangs—but we kept on yelling "Bad dog!" till she didn't, and before Stacy could even walk that well she was already riding around on Lovie's back like a horse, through the yard we never mowed on purpose. My dad had grown a beard, and my mom wore her hair in two braided ropes, like an Indian. My dad never liked any of that hippie shit, but the 60's had their effect on everybody, I guess. We went on long walks through the woods—crossing little streams on rocks that stuck out of the water—and picked apples off the trees. We milked the goat, and drank wine at every dinner. My dad would make a fire and play guitar at nights. He'd play "The Wabash Cannonball." It was some kind of place to live.

Back behind the house there were so many lilac bushes that, from inside, their bloom each spring seemed to fill up every windowpane—all purple and flowery with that candy scent floating all around. It only lasted a real short time, then all the little flowers turned brown and they stank like shit. Let me tell you, my dad should have named that place Lilac Farm.

The animals. There got to be so many animals. And we couldn't take care of them all ourselves, so my dad hired locals to feed them and clean the pens—zit-faced, longhaired kids that wore black T-shirts and smoked pot behind the stable. They didn't like the work so they badmouthed my dad. They told the other locals that we worshipped the devil and that my mom was a witch. Some people didn't believe it though—they thought my dad was in the mafia. Everybody had a theory about us. When my little sister started school she'd come home in the afternoons, running up our long dirt driveway, crying her big blue eyes out. I was in junior high school by then and I'd already learned, whenever I heard kids talking about this weird old house in the middle of the woods, where animals were sacrificed and baby blood was drunk at midnight, not to even bother saying that I lived there and that none of it was true.

And the money. It cost so much to run that place and to pay the *taxes* on it and to fix the things that broke down—water pipes frozen and busted, roof leaking in thirty places at once—that all the cash my dad made from his restaurants disappeared before it was time.

Things started to get very tense as we ran out of money. We couldn't pay the rednecks to lay around and talk crazy shit about us any more, so we had to do all the work. But my mom did most of it. She started taking prescription speed in order to get everything done—the cooking and the cleaning and the taking care of all the animals and us. My sister was too little to help, and I had started high school, and my dad was going around to all the banks to try and get financing to build a restaurant in town. Some nights he came home real late, and some nights he didn't come home at all.

I remember going to pick up our mail at the post office on my bicycle (we couldn't keep a mailbox up for more than a night without some carload of in-breds smashing it all up with baseball bats) and as soon as I walked in the door this postmaster, or mailman, or whatever—this very redfaced, excitable, balding old guy with a white mustache who stood behind the counter—said to me:

"I hear your boss's trying to start himself a restaurant." I guess he thought I was just another employee of my dad's, eager as fuck to slander it up.

"Yeah, that's what I hear," I said, too much a coward, I guess, to tell him who I really was.

"Wail he ain't gettin' no loan, I'll tell you that right now."

"Why's that?" I said real quietly.

"Everybody knows he'll just burn the damn thing down for the insurance just like he did to all them he owned in Chicaga. That's how he made all his damned money. Then he went and blew it all on cocaine, and now he wants to pull the same shit out here. These ain't no Chicaga bankers he's dealin' with now, though."

I just swung open the door to that place and left. I wanted to look around the street and find a brick and throw it through the goddamned plate glass front window of the place, but I didn't. It was getting dark so I just got on my bike and rode home with the mail. None of my dad's restaurants ever burned down. If you go and look today they're all still standing, and they're all still restaurants. I should have told that to the guy, but I didn't.

So he never got the loan, and that final winter that we spent out there got so cold that my mom moved just about all the dogs inside the house with us so they could stay warm too. We didn't have the money to take sick dogs to the vet any more, so I had to just take them—usually carry them in my arms they were so sick —out to the woods and shoot them. (We'd long since gotten the right sized shells for that little shotgun.) And when new litters of pups were born I had to tie them up in sacks of rocks and drown them in a garbage can filled with water. After awhile I didn't even care, but my mom loved all those dogs. That was the difference between her and me—I only loved Lovie.

Pretty soon the kids at school started telling my sister that she smelled bad, and I guess she did, what with living in the same house as thirty dogs. In cages and not. My dad heard about it and he made me kill and bury every one of them except Lovie. That was right before he got arrested.

I was at school when I found out. Read it in the paper while sitting in the library before classes. It was still kind of dark out, so they had all the lights on in the school. It's a very strange thing to walk out of natural darkness into electric light in the middle of the morning. My dad got caught, the night before, trying to bribe a banker into giving him his loan. The phone'd been disconnected that week, so I don't know if he tried to call us or not. I didn't feel a thing when I read it, and I don't even think I felt anything that afternoon when I was walking down a crowded hallway, past the cafeteria, on the way to class, and I heard my name being screamed through the racket all the kids were making. Then there was no more sound, like I'd suddenly gone under water. It was my mom. I knew it was her before I even rounded the corner and saw her there, kicking and screaming while one of my gym teachers held her underneath the armpits and around the neck in a wrestling move so that her feet dangled off the ground while her eyes rolled back into her head, and a strand of spit stretched from her mouth and all the way down to the waxed-up tile of the hallway floor.

I felt for a second like I didn't have any legs, but I didn't fall down. Instead I walked over to her — it felt like I was stepping across a lunar landscape — and wrapped my arms around her waist so they couldn't pull me off. They did pull me off though, but not until her body'd turned ice cold and limp. Eating three months of prescription speed all at once'll do that to a person.

So what happened next? Right?

I remember them half-carrying me to some little room with a desk. There was brown corkboard on the walls. They told me to stay there, and went to get somebody. I didn't stay there, of course — the room was on the first floor and I just climbed out the window and walked home. I remember it being so terribly cold that the wind whistled and my face burned. But aside from that there was no sound or pain or weight or anything for the whole four miles.

When I was nearly home I saw a cop car pull into our driveway. The woods were so thick, and our house was set so far back that you couldn't see it from the road. So I ducked under an old barbed-wire fence and into the woods, and trudged through the snow and between the branches of the apple trees that all hung heavy with white. After about four hundred yards I cold see our house. There were a bunch of cops and men in suits (IRS guys I think) going in and out, some of them carrying my dad's business files and stuff. They stayed the whole day, and so did I, staring at them from the woods and wondering where they'd taken my sister. All I had on was jeans and a sweater and gym shoes and no gloves. To this day my fingers and toes hurt whenever it gets cold out.

Finally they left, and when they did I saw right off that they'd shot Lovie. Right by the front door. She wouldn't let them in, so they shot her. They could have used a knock-out dart or something, but why bother, right? Half her head was caved in and her brains had spilt out into the snow. I went right down to the stable and came back with a wheelbarrow, a shovel, and a pickaxe. I turned the barrow on its side and rolled Lovie's big body in. Then I righted it, and shoveled the bloody snow and brains up on top of her. I remember that I started to cry as I was burying her in the woods by a frozen stream, but I only started. The clay I was digging in was rock solid, and I thought my fingers would break off every time I swung that pickaxe down from over my head with both hands as hard as I could.

After it was done I walked back to the house and broke through the yellow tape the police had put up over our door. It was dark inside, but I could see by the moon that the furniture had been turned over and there were papers scattered everywhere. The electricity'd been shut off, and there was no hot water. There was cooking gas though, so I boiled big kettles of water and poured them into the bathtub until it was full. Then I stripped my wet shoes and socks and wet clothes off and climbed on in.

It might sound very strange but I wasn't thinking about my mom being dead exactly. I wasn't wondering straight out about my dad or where my sister was either. There was just this feeling falling and rising inside me, tightening and relaxing—like everything was over but nothing was settled. I stayed there in the tub, in the dark, until long after the water'd turned ice cold, and then I left and I never came back.

ZACK

Don Gennaro De Grazia

There's an ancient Turkish proverb that goes: the first time you see a man, look into his eyes and you will look into his very soul. The first time I saw Zack Mustafa, he was pissing out a fourth-story window at the Sleepy Bear Motel down on Canal, and his eyes were closed.

The Sleepy Bear is the no-star flophouse where all Chicago-area military recruits are ordered to stay the night before they're shipped across the country to various boot camps. After the judge told Tim and I to join the service or go to jail, we signed up for the Illinois Army National Guard (Infantry), which meant we were headed for four months of basic training at Fort Benning, Georgia. Like a couple of conscripted Catholics on the night before Lent, Tim and I brought two cases of beer, two fifths of Jack, and found ourselves two Filipino Navy nurses-to-be who were staying down on the second floor, and in the same boat as us, so to speak. Now, the mathematics of the situation would seem simple: there were two of us and two of everything else, right? As usual Tim's rawboned magnetism defied all laws of logic, and, as he and the two aspiring Florence Nightingales started getting silly together—wrestling and tickling and unzipping and unclasping—on one of the twin beds, I forlornly slunk out the door with both of the fifths.

As I made my way out of the Filipinos' room and back towards mine and Tim's up on the fourth floor—up the dingy back staircase, and down the long, smelly, dimly-lit hallway which lay before me like a green-shag-carpeted El tunnel—I saw a young guy's profile as he pissed out a window and into the darkness below. To my drunken, soreheaded sensibilities, this dark and hawk-nosed character was not simply urinating out a window, he was making the ultimate swashbuckler statement.

"Move over," I said, as I walked up next to him, set one of the fifths down on the sill, and unzipped my fly. "And remember," I said, glancing down at the blacktop of the empty parking lot below, "do not, under any circumstances, cross the streams."

That perked his interest. His blackish eyes flew open and flashed with some strange mix of naiveté and menace.

"Why not?" There was something very little-kid-like about the way he asked that.

"Because . . ." I said, "because, to cross the streams might very possibly throw the entire universe off its axis."

"Whaddya mean—'off its axis'?" he asked me dubiously, shifting his cock with his hand so that the streams, until then parallel, now X'd a few feet in front of us, before continuing and eventually fraying and splashing into the parking lot, several yards short of the dark and empty street.

"Now you've done it," I said, setting down the other fifth and placing my palm against the window frame, as if bracing for the downfall of the cosmos.

From seemingly nowhere I heard a deep voice boom:

"Hey y'all watch where yer pissin'!" Before I could locate the source Zack was already yelling back.

"What are you worried about? You're on the other side of the street, loser."

So I looked to the other side of the street and saw them emerging from the shadows that a big brick building threw down on the sidewalk, and into the light of the street lamp: four or five born-big hickish types, all decked out in their best mesh T-shirts and skin-tight acid-washed jeans, and all looking up at us with their chests inflated and thrown out, and, I'd imagine, the hair on the back of their red necks bristling with rural indignation.

"Awww shucks, whatsammatter fellas?" I asked, as they crossed the street towards our window, while Zack and I redeposited our members and zipped up. "Where y'all from—Iowa? Y'all get lost on the way to Clark and Division? Shucks . . ."

They shouted up at me, shaking their fists. I laughed and, with a four-story height advantage, told them to bring it on—dramatically tilting my head back and drinking down several healthy gulps from the already two-thirds-empty bottle of whiskey for good measure.

A couple hours later I was laying on my back in mine and Tim's room, reeling, the empty bottle of Jack laying somewhere on the floor on its side, talking non-stop to Tim who'd finally come back up to our room from his marathon Filipino screw-fest. As usual, he went about his business—getting undressed, washing his face—and acted like he wasn't even listening to me.

"This fucking guy's method of argumentation was fucking cracking me up, man. I mean, all these steroid-eating hillbillies yelling up how they'll rip our fucking . . . and this guy's yelling back shit like: 'You're not even from this community and now you're citing community standards? Do we come down to Iowa and complain when you guys marry your sisters and fuck goats up the ass?' And they're like kicking newspaper boxes and yelling, 'We're not from eye-o-wah! Whon' choo come on down here an' we'll whup yer asses. Sheeeeit. Yahoo!'

"And this guy—*Zack*—this guy Zack says: 'There's five, no six of you, and two of us, how can you fuckers honestly expect us to come down there you fucking cretins?' And the biggest guy, this—he looked like a skin, Tim, boots and bald but he was just a big jock hick I'm telling you—he points up at Zack and says 'Just me and you motherfucker.' And Zack goes: 'O.K., I'll come down just as soon as you tell all your GAY LOVERS to leave!' And they're like: 'You're the gay ones playing piss games!' and Zack's like 'Yeah right, why don't you take that ceramic dildo outta your ass and then talk.'

"So the big guy's really pissed and he tells all his friends to leave and they start walking down the street towards the Post Office and Zack yells down: 'Nice try fuckers, I'm not coming down unless you go over there, and he's pointing in the opposite direction, so they start jogging in that direction and he's leaning out over the windowsill going 'No, over *there*', so they stop and start running in the opposite direction, and he's like 'No, over there,' and the big guy who just stood there the whole time grabs one of his buddies' arms real pissed and they all stop and start swearing and yelling unintelligible shit like: 'rrrrraaaaaarrrffuckyu!'

"So I'm like: 'Come up here then tough guys,' and out of the corner of my mouth I'm telling Zack they got the whole place under lock-down, and they're like, 'We'll be up there you fuckers.' So they start trying all the doors and they're all locked, and then they disappear around the back and we start laughing and drinking. I ended up drinking that whole fifth myself. So we're laughing and shit and all of the sudden we hear this commotion stomping up the back stairway and me and Zack look at each other like: SHIT! and we start running down the hall towards the room and I can't find my keys so we just start trying every doorknob and they're all locked except for one and it's this fucking closet with, like, linen hampers and maid shit, so we go in there but it's so small that we can't shut the door all the way—it's still open a couple of inches so I can see them when they all pour into the hallway looking for us and I start laughing and Zack's like 'Shut up' so I do and they all run right past us and up to the window and start saying what pussies we are for leaving and blah, blah, and they leave.

"So as soon as they're gone Zack runs back to the window and waits until he sees them in the street again and yells: 'Hey you fucking faggots—where were you?' And they say: 'We just waint up thur!' And Zack's like: 'This is the fourth floor. The . . . fourth . . . floor. Can't you count?' And he sticks his hands out the window and starts showing them on his fingers—1, 2, 3, 4. 'What're you all from Iowa or something?' And they're all like 'RRRarrrrr! You fuhkers!' and they start running back around the building but some security guy comes around the corner and tells them to beat it and we're like 'Yeah, losers, beat it! Hahahhahaha!'

"And get this man, this Zack guy's infantry. Fort Benning. He'll be with us the whole four months."

Right, then I felt Tim grab me by me sweat-soaked T-shirt and yank me up to a sitting position. When I opened my eyes the room was teetering and Tim's face and upper body were half-lit by the red glow of the alarm clock next to me.

"Listen," he said, "we gotta get through this thing without any fucking problems! Stay away from that guy. You hear me? He's trouble."

Imagine the whole situation, if you will: I'm tanked out of my mind and Tim's got me by the shirt. He himself is shirtless, so that all his tattoos are showing: his blue spider web on the elbow, his green and red dragon all across the left side of his chest, the rest of his skin crawling with various spiders and scorpions and skulls, and actual blood's dripping from all these cat scratches that the Filipinos left on him while he fucked them both. This big, bloody, tattooed, skinheaded, sex-smelling, whiskey-breathed motherfucker is looking me in the eye and saying: "Stay away from that guy—he's trouble." I burst out laughing so hard that I started puking all over myself, and Tim threw me back down on the bed and started laughing too: at me and at himself.

Then the alarm went off—it was 3:55 in the morning. Over the course of the next week, while they shipped us and processed us and measured us and fitted us and filled in all the free time with little games aimed at breaking us down and building us up brand-new, I'll bet I got no more than a total of ten hours sleep. That hangover lasted, I swear to god, until four months later when we were all on a plane —Tim and Zack and I in our class A greens and cunt-caps—headed back to Chicago without an inkling of what the hell we were going to do with our lives. Well, that went for me and Tim anyway—Zack had a few ideas.

THE ROGUE SCHOLARS

Don Gennaro De Grazia

> The music almost died away . . . then burst like a pent-up flood;
> And it seemed to say, "Repay! Repay!" and my eyes were blind with blood.
> The thought came back of an ancient wrong, and it stung like a frozen lash,
> And the lust awoke to kill, to kill . . . then the music stopped with a crash.
>
> "The Shooting of Dan McGrew"
—Robert Service

The night Zack brought home the stunguns I was in my bedroom chanting, because, well, I was Buddhist. Or at least I was when I chanted.

It was great—sitting there crosslegged in front of the little shrine, waves of sandalwood incense hitting me every so often, an apple and banana lying perfectly, like the model for a still-life, in a glass bowl, underneath the scroll of Chinese Sanskrit characters that hung from a naked presswood box I'd screwed to the wall. It sounds goofy, but that night, and every night that I chanted, my twelve-by-twelve-foot square of a room—lined on all four walls with shelves of books—seemed like the only thing I'd ever need to get everything I'd ever wanted. And all the hatreds inside of me (and there were a lot, I'll tell you) soothed on down like I guess a black eye's supposed to do when you slap a raw beefsteak on it.

Halfway through that evening's *Gongyo* I heard the front door to the Rogue Palace open and close, as someone walked in and stood in front of my door, listening to me chant. Then, Zack—I knew it couldn't be anyone else but him—started chanting along with me in a voice, muffled by the door, that purposely sounded like a retarded deaf person:

"NAm Myo hO rEnGAYY!"

I paused for a second, really pissed off, and tried to think of something incredibly clever to say to him. Something short and mean that would totally destroy his world, which basically consisted of doomed schemes to get rich and get laid. But the Buddha mood got the better of me and I let it pass.

I wondered what he was up to, though. I always wondered what he was up to. So I cut my evening chant-fest short—striking the tiny, but resounding, bowl-bell that sat on the floor beside me—and went into the hallway to see.

Zack was standing there dressed in his typical duds—a black polo and a pair of baggy pleated khakis, with one of those black leather hip sacks belted around his waist: centered so that it hung over his crotch like a protective cup. He was trying to look at the back of his head in the hallway mirror.

"Hey friend," he said, looking at me as I shut my bedroom door, "shave my neck?"

When he and I and Tim had been in the Army, we would take turns shaving each other before inspection in the field, where there were no mirrors or shaving cream —just dull razors and canteen water. Though Tim had started growing his hair out, Zack and I kept our close-cropped high-and-tights. So the you-shave-me-I'll-shave-you tradition continued. At least for the back of our necks. It was cheaper than going to the barber once a week—thrice a week in Zack's case, dark and hairy hawk-nosed dog of a Turkish-German that he was.

As I lathered up the back of his neck that night and scraped the yellow disposable Bic in strips that ran down from the base of his skull to almost where his spine started, the phone rang. I went and answered it. It was Zack's mom.

"Zack!" I said, and then whispered, more than loud enough for her to hear, "Get that needle out of your arm, dude—it's your *mom*."

Zack squeezed his eyes shut and screwed his face into a grimaced smile.

"Thanks, friend," he said.

I could hear Zack's mom babbling at him from a hundred miles away. And though she screamed in Turkish, I knew the basic topics she was exploring: Zack's horrendous grades, his younger brother's and sister's horrendous grades, his drinking, pot smoking, drug dealing, the tainted future that his misdeeds had ensured him, and, in general, the fact that manic-depressive behavior was inherited. That diagnosis had been Zack's father's, two years before, when he was the youngest District Judge in Illinois, until he stuck the barrel of a 9-mm pistol in his mouth and pulled the trigger, thus ending his reign.

As Zack listened and nodded, Tim suddenly burst in through the door with a briefcase. He barely gave me a nod before heading down the hall to his room. I'd seen very little of him as of late—he was buying food stamps from the local gangbangers who'd been taking them in exchange for drugs, and then reselling them to a crooked Jewel manager. He'd invited me in on the scam, but what were loads of dirty money compared to the joys of arduous prayer? It pissed him off that I wanted no part of it. I could tell.

"Ma . . ." I hard Zack say, "Ma, I know. I gotta go. I've gotta GO! Alex is confused about his sexuality and there's some gay hotline he wants to call."

He hung up and immediately addressed me:

"Friend," he said, "we're winning."

"Whaddya mean 'we're winning'?"

"Scored us some zappers, friend."

Then, with half his neck still covered with shaving cream, Zack walked purposefully into the living room followed by Scud—our highly disappointing pit bull —and an obviously curious Alex Verdi. Zack stepped behind the bar and produced two black electrical devices about the size and shape of a deodorant stick, and lay them on the formica for my perusal. Two short, silver prongs jutted out of the top end of each one.

Zack then picked one of them up, fitted his fingers into the molded grooves that ran along one side, and pressed a small button near the top with his thumb. A tiny blue bolt of electricity flickered and crackled between the two silver prongs. He stepped out from behind the bar and touched the live spikes to one of our metal folding chairs, which immediately became the host of something like a mini-electrical storm, what with those blue flickering currents dancing and jumping across the entire frame.

"Whoa!" I said, taking a surprised step back in spite of myself. "Jesus," I said.

Zack knew that, for me, this moment was akin to a mad scientist seeing an abstract idea suddenly materialize before him out of thin air.

"If only there were some way to keep from getting fucked with without having to kill the person," I had often mused.

It turned out there was a way—the PowerJak Stungun—and now, I thought, as I carefully fondled one, at long last these wonderful weapons were finally in the right hands.

"Where'd you *get* these?" I asked.

"I traded Chang twelve hits of liquid and a gram of weed," Zack said. Chang was a Korean acid-eating weapons freak of a computer engineering major that Zack knew from school.

"Do they work?" I asked. He was obviously a little disappointed at the question.

"I don't know, friend," he admitted.

"Fuck, I'll bet they don't work," I said. For the next couple of minutes we discussed all the possible ways of finding out the stungun's effectiveness. I seemed to Zack, though, that every time he made a reasonable suggestion, I would veer around it by making a joke.

"Think. Who could we zap?" he asked.

"How 'bout Scud—next time he pisses on the rug?" I answered. At the mention of his name he looked up stupidly with close-set eyes, bumping his cement-block head on the folding chair.

"I mean, if he'd at least lift his leg when he does it," I added, but Zack persisted.

"Look," I finally said, "we can't just go and zap some loser unprovoked."

"There's nobody?"

"No," I said.

Then I heard Tim's voice. He was standing right behind me. He said:

"Not even Dembinsky?"

Less than ten minutes later we were boarding the northbound Howard El train at Morse. It was an extremely dark, cool summer night, and it continued to get cooler as Zack and Tim and I got off at Howard and walked north, past the CTA yard where the El trains sleep at night, and past the sprawled-out Calvary Cemetery that separates the relatively wealthy neighborhood of South Evanston from the paint-peeling back porches of Rogers Park Chicago, and towards the renovated loft apartment where Dembinsky and Carrie now lived.

Twenty minutes later we were standing in a back alley behind the old six-story Marshall Field's building which had been remodeled for the purpose of housing hip young professionals—like Dembinsky, for instance, who now worked at the Board of Trade, while his new love, Carrie (my Carrie), finished up graduate school and taught aerobics. Now, I say "my Carrie," because she had once been mine, and would still be mine today, mine in eternal bliss and all that, were it not for the fact that Dembinsky had betrayed me, taken Carrie, and nearly gotten my ass—as well as Zack's and Tim's asses—thrown in prison, all in one shitty swoop.

"Ah, well—all's fair in love and war," you say? Exactly, exactly.

In the shadows of a lone steel lamp that hung above the concrete loading dock, surrounded by overflowing dumpsters and stacks of wooden slats, Zack and Tim formulated a plan while my initial anger subsided and I began to have second thoughts.

From Dembinsky's fourth-floor address, which I had long ago procured for the purpose of, among other things, knowing which door to knock on when I finally mustered up the moral mandate (i.e., courage) to kill the bastard, Tim determined which window was to be our Normandy. To his and Zack's joy it was positioned within reach of the vaulted roof of the shorter, adjoining building—the old Victory Theater.

Zack was a notorious climber of things. As he shot up the brick siding of the Victory building like a spider and reached the black grating of the fire escape, the sureness with which he acted seemed to suggest strongly that he'd done this all before. As I pondered that thought, I suddenly realized that I wanted out. Questions began arising as to the justness of the act we were about to commit. And self-preservation instincts chimed in as well when Zack suddenly dropped the bottom section of the fire escape to the alley floor with a clatter.

"Hey c'mon!" Zack yelled down at me as I bolted for a hiding place. "C'mon . . . nobody lives here, it's all stores."

"Even up there?" I whispered, pointing towards the third-floor windows of the former theater.

"No. They were making it into apartments and then some bums snuck in and started a fire to keep warm. Gutted the whole place. C'mon."

"Yeah, get up there, ya girl," Tim said, suddenly reaching out with both hands and stretching a nylon stocking over my head. "I'll stay down here and look out and shit."

So I stepped onto the bottom rung and climbed up towards Zack, who was now climbing on top of the vaulted aluminum-and-tar roof. Once I got up there and he saw my nylon-smashed face, he pulled a balled-up black ski mask from his pocket and put it on. Together, with a PowerJak clipped to each of our belts, we climbed the slippery arch of a roof and counted the windows of the old Marshall Field's building that lay before us on the horizon.

A couple yards before the two buildings actually met, the roof we stood on dropped off—five or six feet—to another level. This formed a little corridor that ran between the lengths of the two buildings.

"That should be it right there," said Zack, pointing to the tops of a row of windows that peaked above the drop-off. All that money they must have been paying to live there, and their view was a brick wall of the adjoining building.

"That window on the far end should be the living room," said Zack. "The one in the middle is the bedroom, and then that little one on the other side is the bathroom."

"How the fuck do you know?"

"I'm just guessing."

We walked gingerly to the edge of the roof and then lowered ourselves down into the corridor, in a spot where there were no windows, only pipes and one steaming tin duct of some sort that protruded from the bricks. Nearly the entire building was darkened, but the second window from the end, Dembinsky and Carrie's bedroom window, was lit.

"What the fuck?" I whispered, "Doesn't he have to work in the morning? It's almost three. Let's go."

"C'mon man," Zack said. So we continued. As we crept towards the window the sounds of music could be heard, the skeleton of which was the basic marching beat of a bass drum. But the song was flushed full of studio sounds—guitar riffs, bass lines, trumpet blasts—to heighten the intensity of the mood. Three men spit out comically machismo rhyming couplets with the beat, and between stanzas a female singer's alluringly high-pitched voice could be heard—first yelping alarmedly, then settling into a satisfied, growling moan:

"Hey!

Hey!

Hey-ee-hey-ee-hey-yeahhh . . ."

Over it all, though, real-life, non-recorded human sounds could be heard (a guy's and a girl's) and the sounds they made—the pants and the gasps and the groans —were the unmistakable strains of lovemaking.

Zack got to the window first and peered in. He immediately turned to me, as I crouched there, frozen, and whispered, with amused sympathy:

"Ohhh, friend, he's got her in the Jody Davis."

What he meant by that was that Dembinsky was lying on his back in bed, while Carrie squatted over him and impaled herself on his stiff penis. Jody Davis was a catcher for the Chicago Cubs. The Rogue Scholars were fond of creating their own slang.

I slapped my hand across my eyes and hung my head, as if to say, "I can't look." But, of course, I did look. By the time I'd wedged myself to the left of Zack, though, Carrie was no longer in the Jody Davis position. She was stretched over the end of the bed, lying on her stomach, while Dembinsky rammed into her from behind. The sight of his ridiculously enlarged powerlifter's buttocks clenching, and his rippling thigh muscles flexing with each thrust, along with his giant's chest, which remained fully expanded as he bridged his upper body over her in a push-up position, made Carrie's tiny, prostrate body seem all the more lean and all the more beautiful to me. I was beyond help.

I felt Zack gently tap me on the shoulder, and turned to see him nod towards the picture windows of the living room, further on down the corridor, which were open in invitation.

"Now?" he asked.

I shook my head and pointed to the shoulder-high bathroom window, which was also open.

"He'll have to piss sometime. I'll just lean in and fuck him up when he does." Zack thought for a second.

"Will the stream of his piss ground him to the toilet water and kill him or something?" Zack asked.

"Do you think I give a fuck?" I hissed, staring hard as Dembinsky's thick, ruddy penis continued to saw in and out of Carrie's pale thighs.

For the next half-hour or so, while the bedroom scene before us rapidly turned into a flip-through of an illustrated copy of the Kama Sutra, I could not help but think back to a time when Carrie was my girl and Dembinsky was merely a born-big frat-boy thug that The Rogue Scholars sold drugs to.

I was brought out of these recollections by the intensity of the grinding couple's lovemaking, as Dembinsky approached orgasm. He grasped Carrie by her slender hips and began simultaneously pulling her towards him as he slammed into her. Amid an interweaving chorus of "Omigod" and "Yes . . . slam into me," and "Nnngggghhyaa!" Dembinsky finally clenched every muscle in his blood-filled arsenal and climaxed, collapsing sweatily on top of her. Their wet bodies—his dark red and hers pale white—looked, in the way that they lay molded together, like layers of clay exposed by strip-mining. They lay like this for less than a minute before Carrie spoke, almost scoldingly, in her ever-raspy voice.

"Get it out!" she said.

Dembinsky at once pulled himself out of her and up to his knees on the queen-sized mattress. He looked down at his still erect penis and stroked the skin of it with an odd expression, as if trying to remember something. Then the look turned to blank realization as he saw that the head of his member had broken through the end of the condom, which was bunched up near the base of his shaft like a translucent yellow garter belt.

Carrie, still face-down underneath him, seemed to sense his dismay.

"What?" she said, rolling over, "What? Oh shit! What the hell is your problem? Why didn't you say something?"

"Ohhh . . ." she cried, scrambling off the bed and racing towards the bathroom. "Shit!"

I knelt outside their window transfixed as Dembinsky stretched out face-down on the mattress and sighed heavily, when the sound of running water suddenly mixed in with the disco music that still filled the room.

Without thinking, I stood up and looked in the bathroom window at Carrie. She was lying on her back in the bathtub—legs splayed straight up in the air like a V, as a powerful rush of water splashed against her vagina, in some wild attempt to flush Dembinsky's seed out of her body.

Carrie continued to bemoan the situation, and to curse Dembinsky, though her words were now inaudible. I watched her for a few minutes and thought of Dembinsky lying there in the next room. The vengeance inside me shriveled up and died, for the moment, flaccidly, in the pit of my stomach. I turned to Zack and nearly cried out with shock to see that he was gone.

I turned to the bedroom window just in time to see him creep into the room and approach the still naked Dembinsky with the stungun. Dembinsky was lying lengthwise on the bed, eyes closed, with one arm tucked underneath his stomach. As Zack reached the foot of the bed, he may have made a slight noise, because Dembinsky raised his head from the pillows for a split second before Zack reached down and stabbed the dull prongs against the smooth, hairless back of Dembinsky's thigh.

Zack pulled the trigger, and for the next four or five seconds Dembinsky seemed to cling to the bed with both his hands and his feet, while his midsection rose and fell and rose and fell in a motion not that unlike, say, an inchworm on a treadmill, if you can imagine such a thing.

Then Zack turned and fled as (I'm sure I imagined this) two threadlike billows of smoke seemed to rise from the motionless Dembinsky's thigh.

Seconds later Zack's leg appeared from the living-room window, and then Zack himself. I rose, and with one final look at Carrie, still lying on her back in the tub muttering to herself, quickly followed after him, up across the slippery roof of the theater and down the fire escape, where Tim stood watch. The three of us ran through the back alleys that led to Wilson's pancake house. I'd made sure to bring my key. Being the underpaid night-manager of a greasy-spoon N.U. hangout was not *completely* without its perks.

Later, guilts and fears and uncertainties over what we did would creep into my mind. But for that moment, as me and Zack and Tim sat hunched over in the darkness of the back storage room, with the door safely locked behind us, my own convulsive laughter bounced off the walls around me, and it sounded like the laughter of a man who was truly alive.